Alphabets & Numbers FOR KIDS

Nora Artchan

AF485609

THIS BOOK BELONGS TO

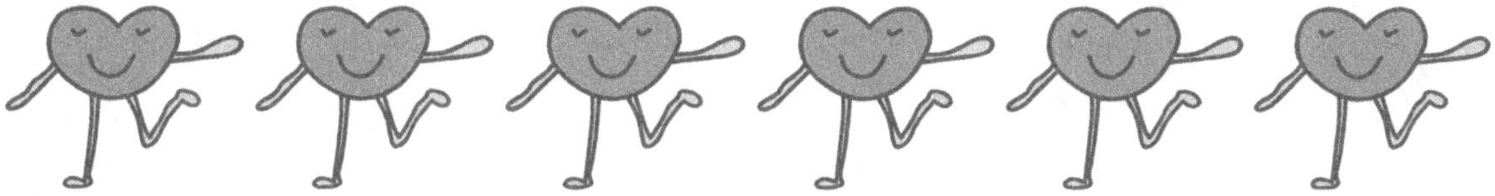

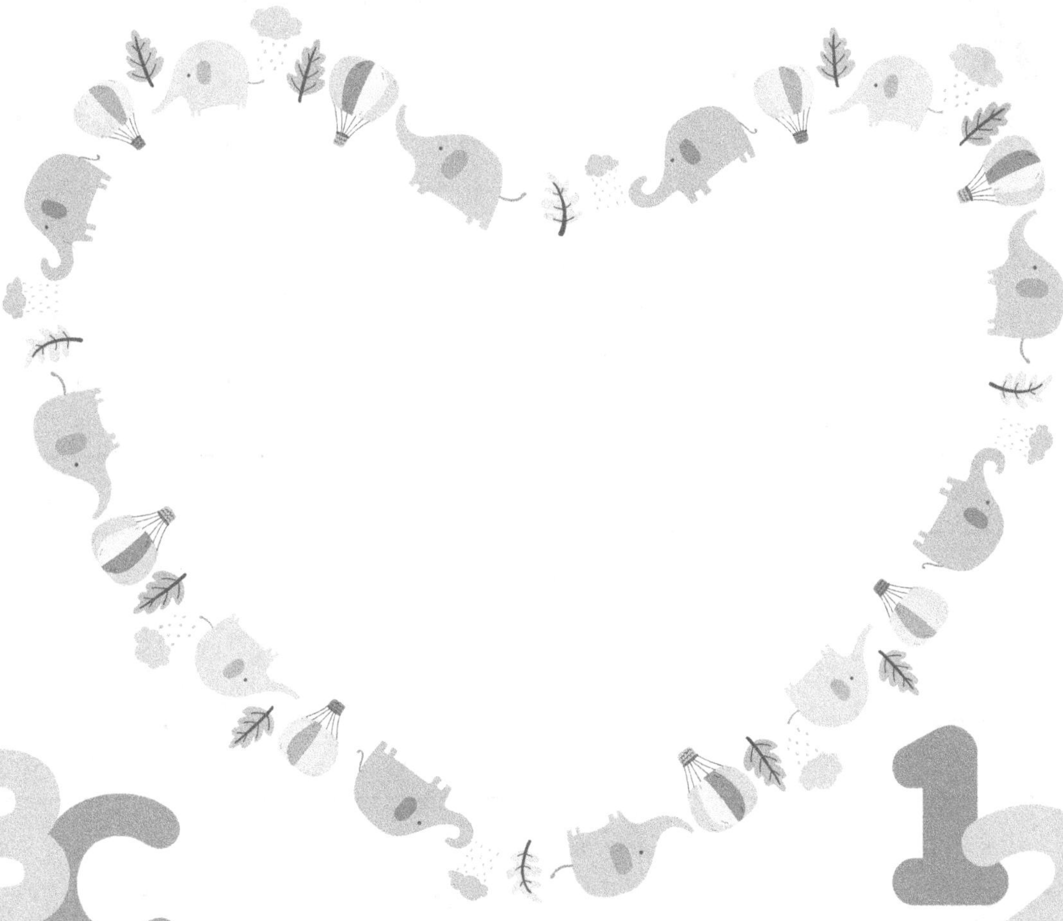

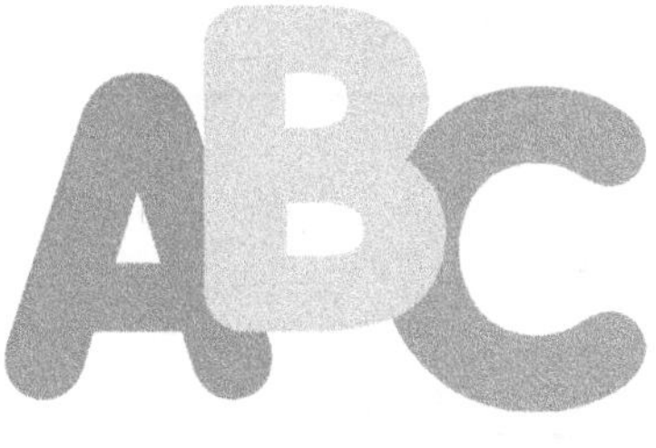

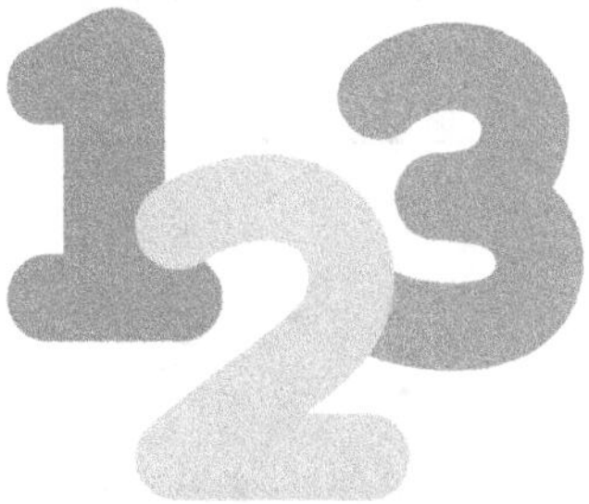

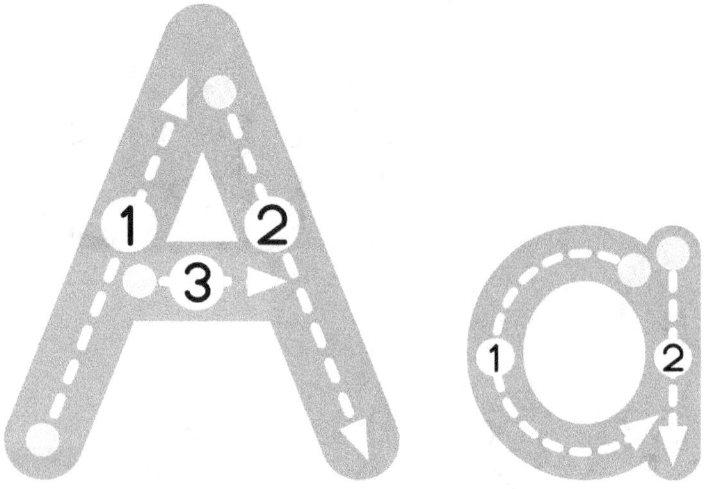

A is for........
Alligator
Angel
Apple
Ant
Ambulance

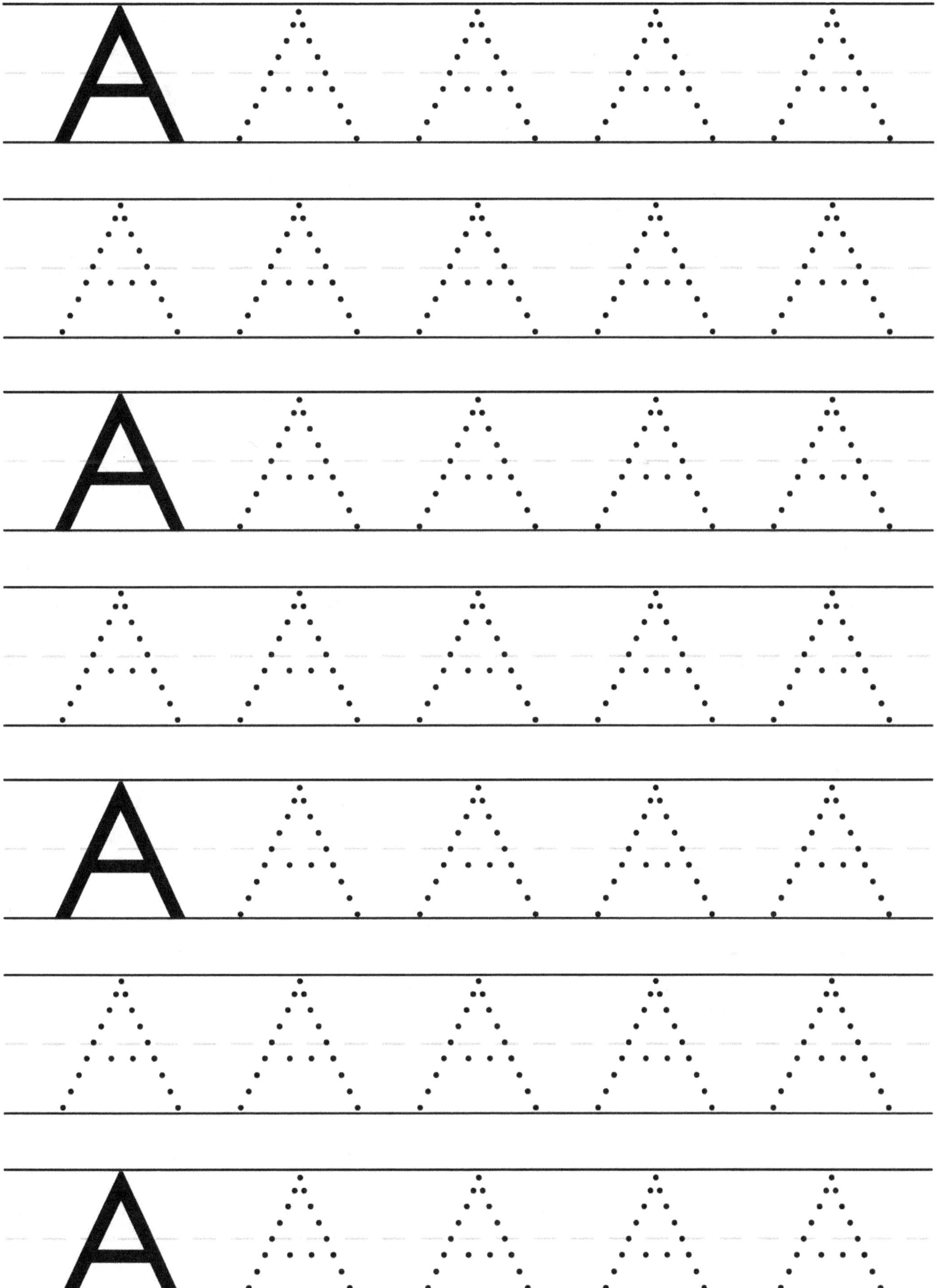

a a a a a a
a a a a a a
a a a a a a
a a a a a a
a a a a a a
a a a a a a

B is for.........

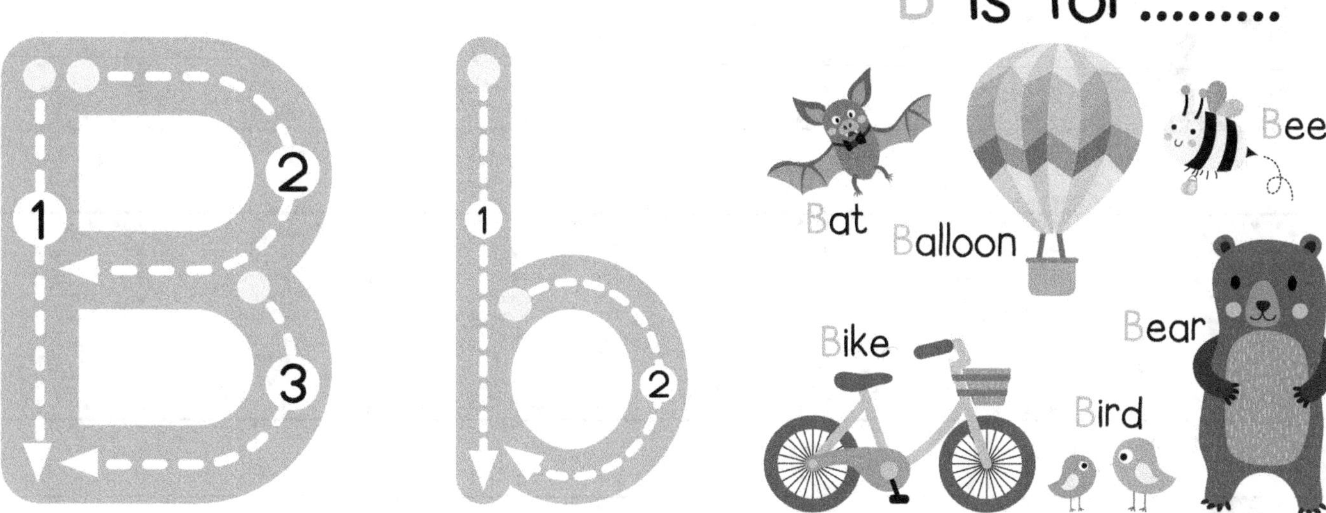

B

B

b

b

B B B B B B
B B B B B B
B B B B B B
B B B B B B
B B B B B B
B B B B B B

b b b b b b

b b b b b b

b b b b b b

b b b b b b

b b b b b b

b b b b b b

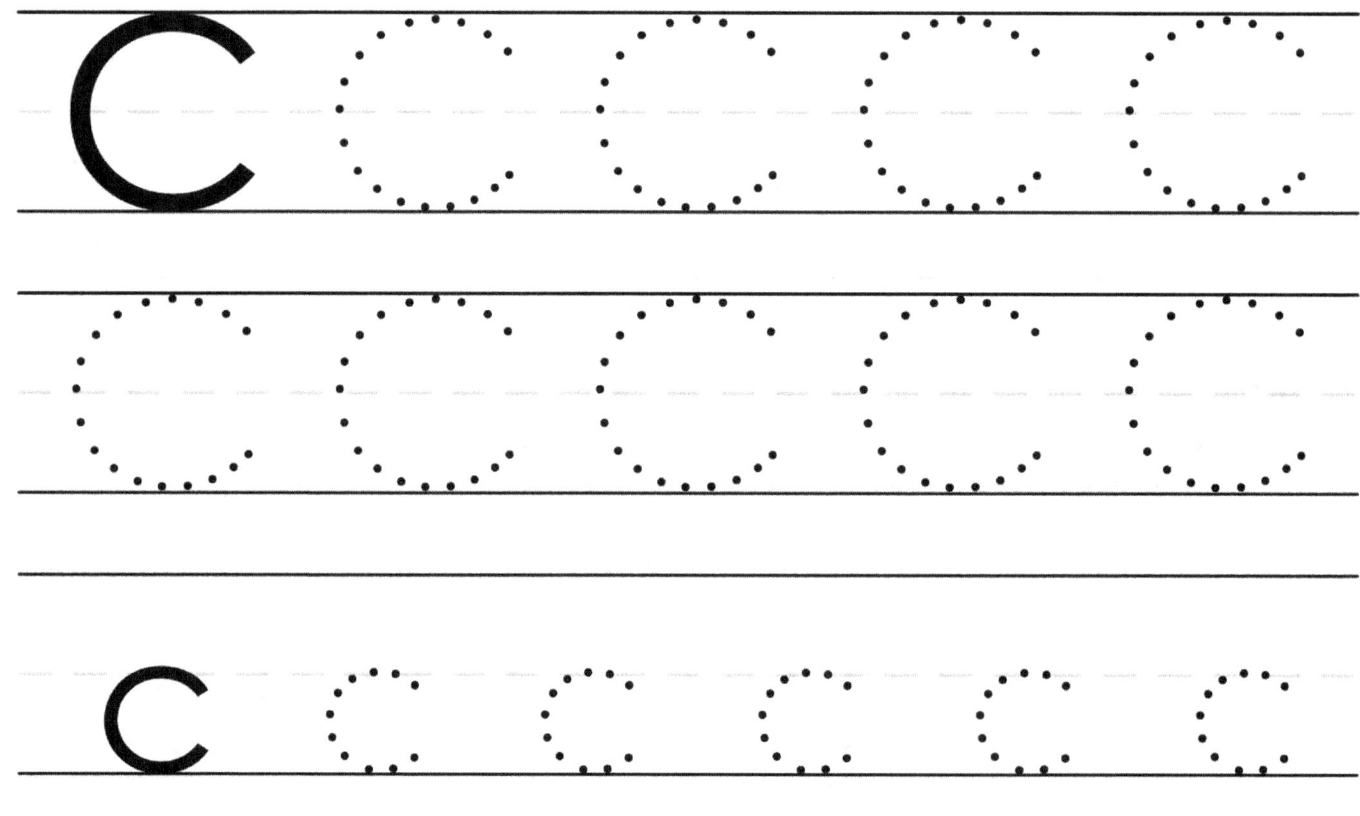

C
C
C

C C C C C
C C C C C
C C C C C
C C C C C
C C C C C
C C C C C

C C C C C C

C C C C C C

C C C C C C

C C C C C C

C C C C C C

C C C C C C

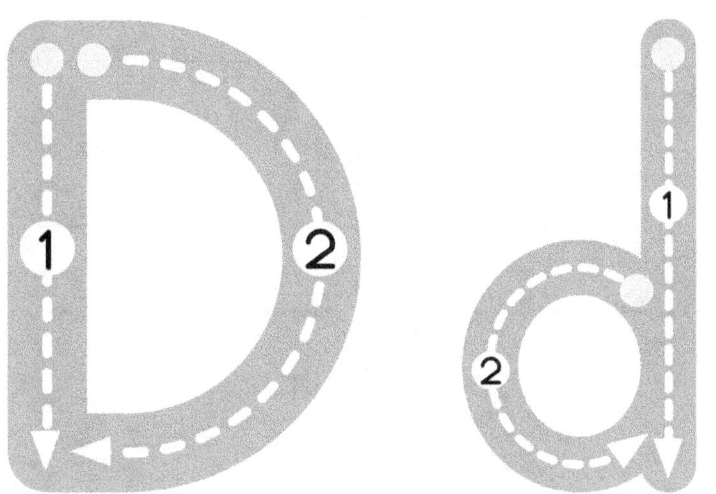

D D D D D D D

D D D D D D D

d d d d d d d

d d d d d d d

D

D

D

d d d d d d

d d d d d d

d d d d d d

d d d d d d

d d d d d d

d d d d d d

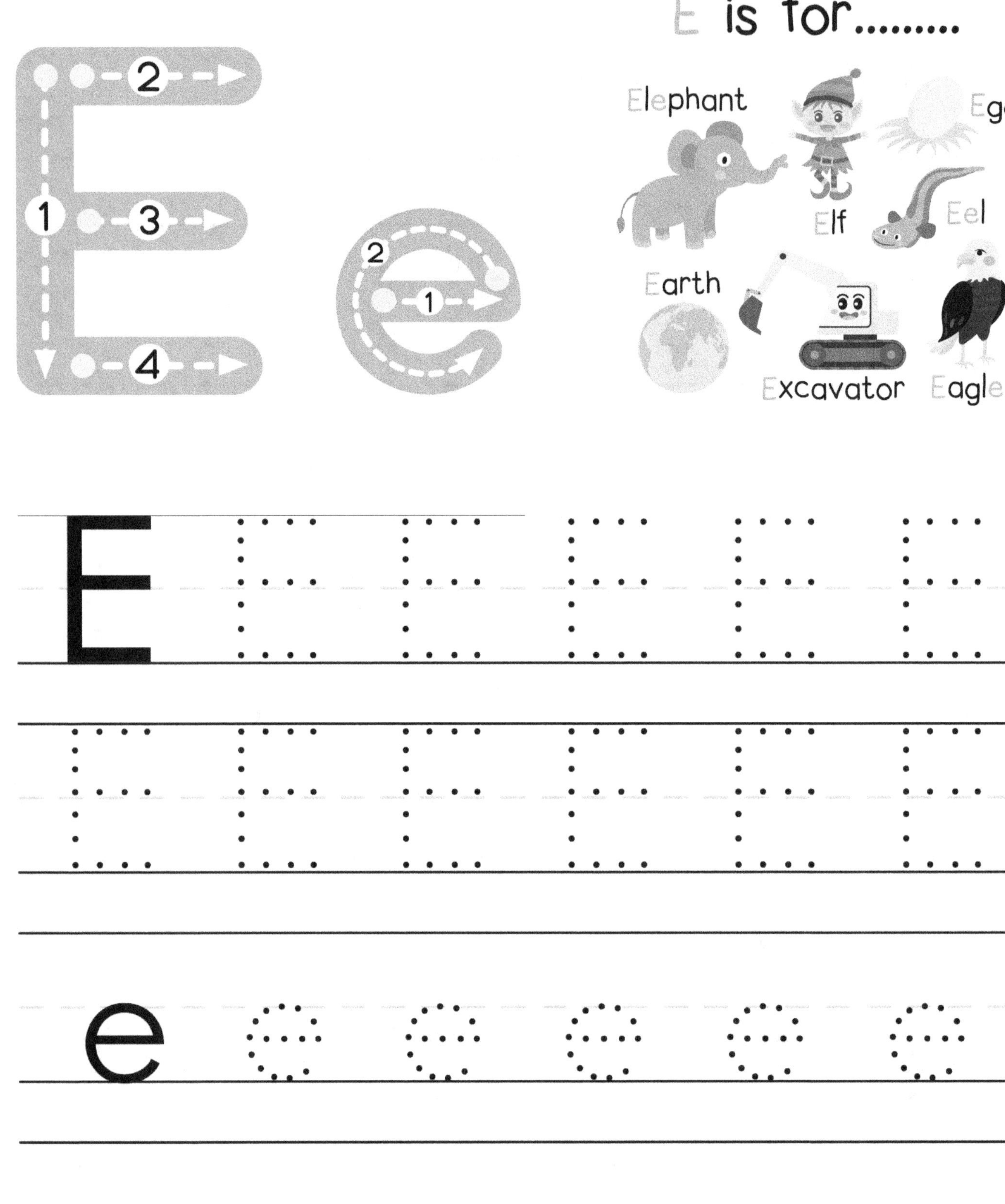

E is for.........
Elephant
Egg
Elf
Eel
Earth
Excavator
Eagle

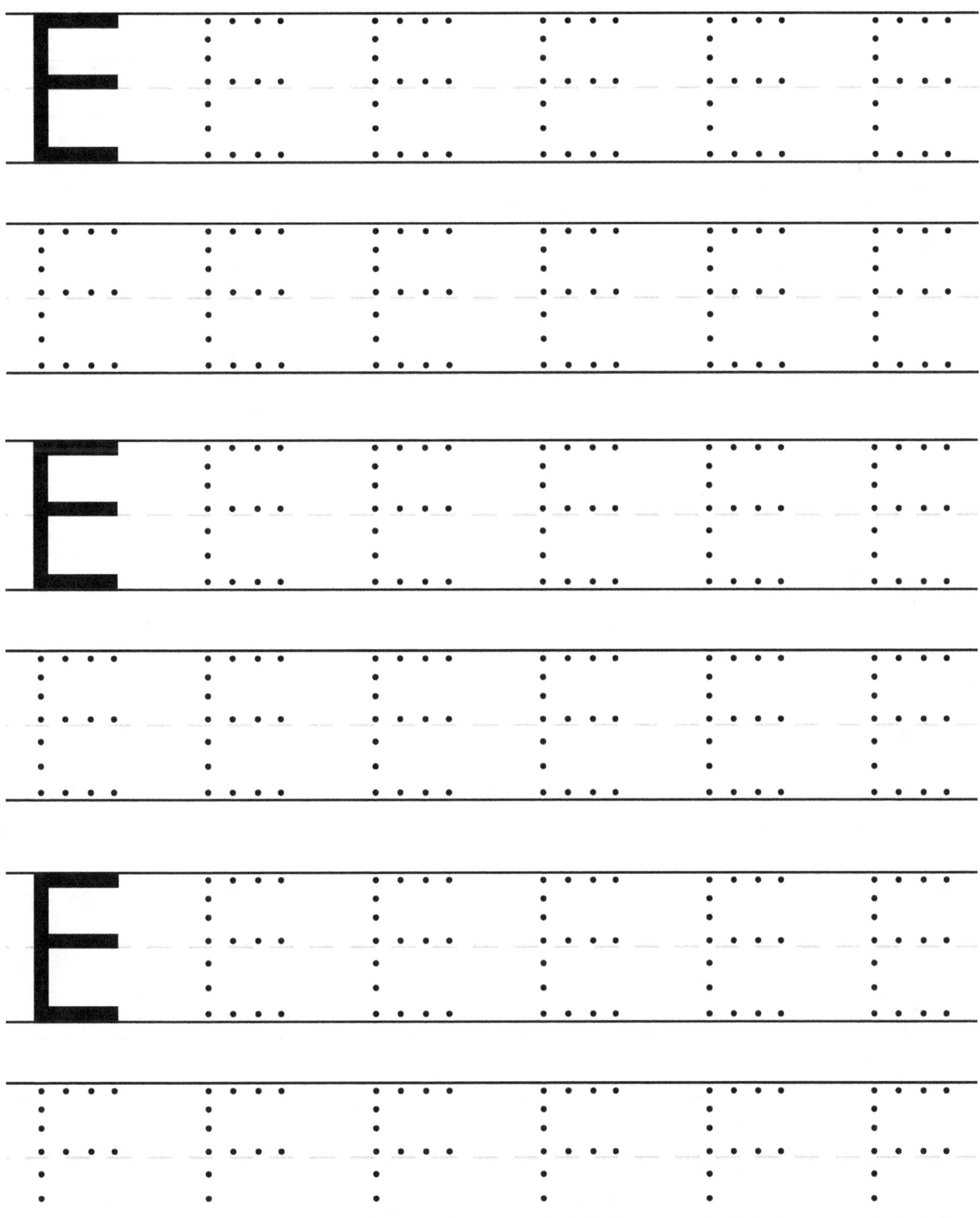

e

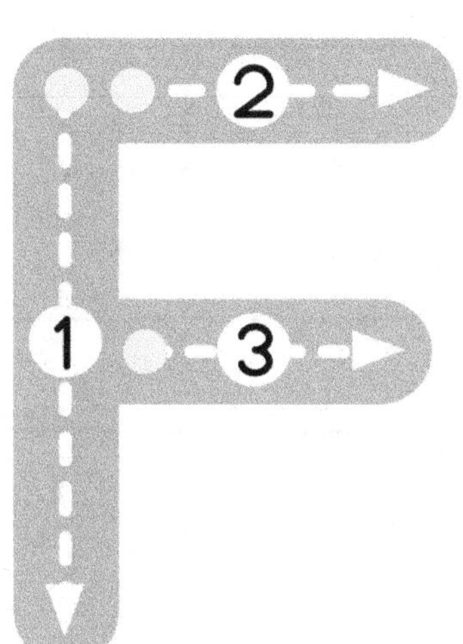

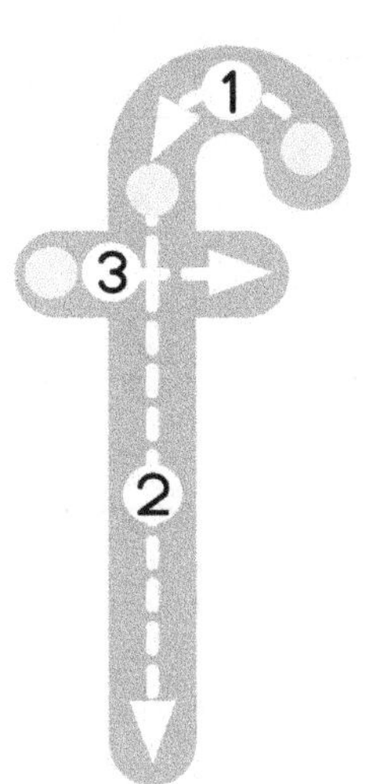

F

f

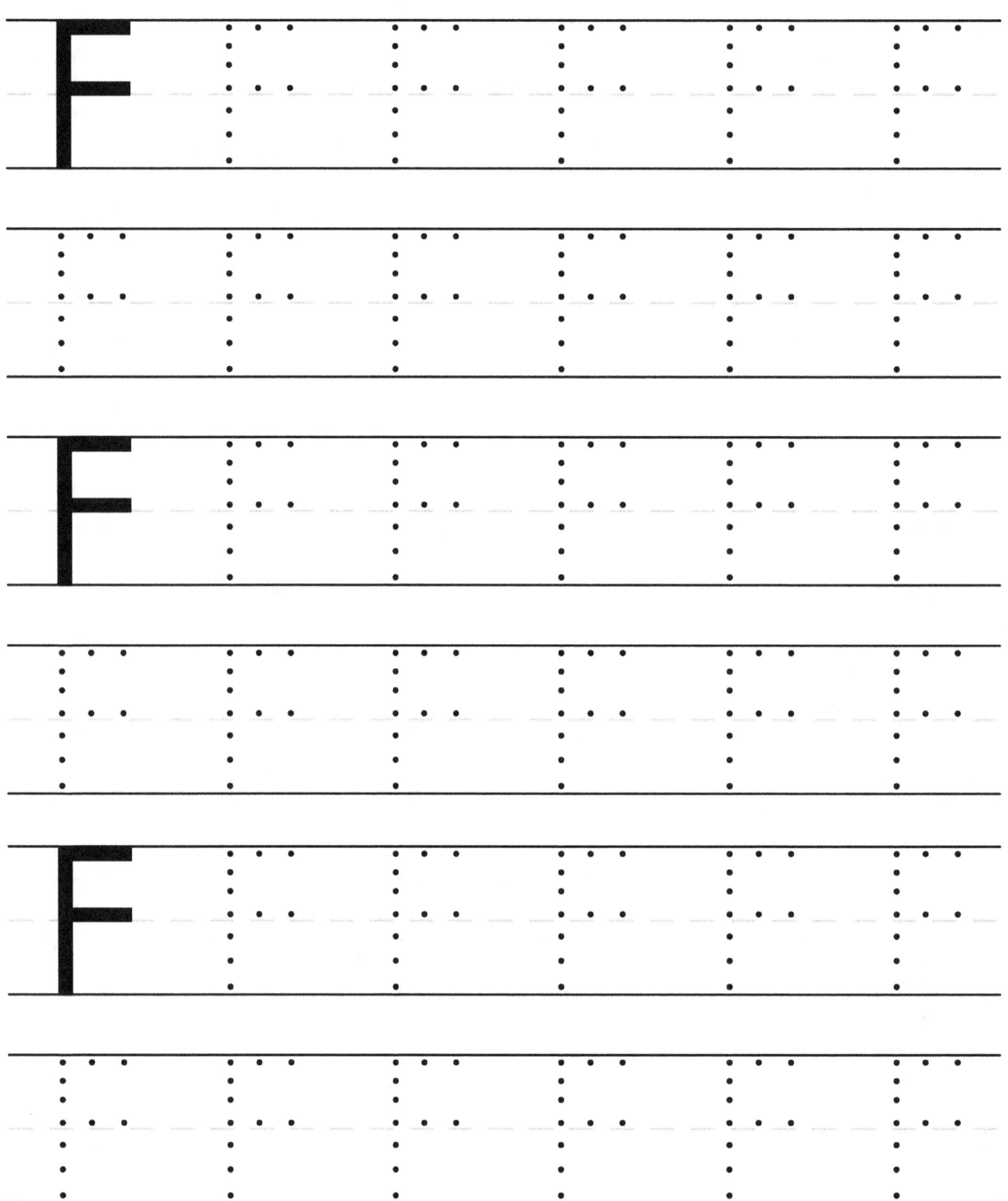

f

f

f

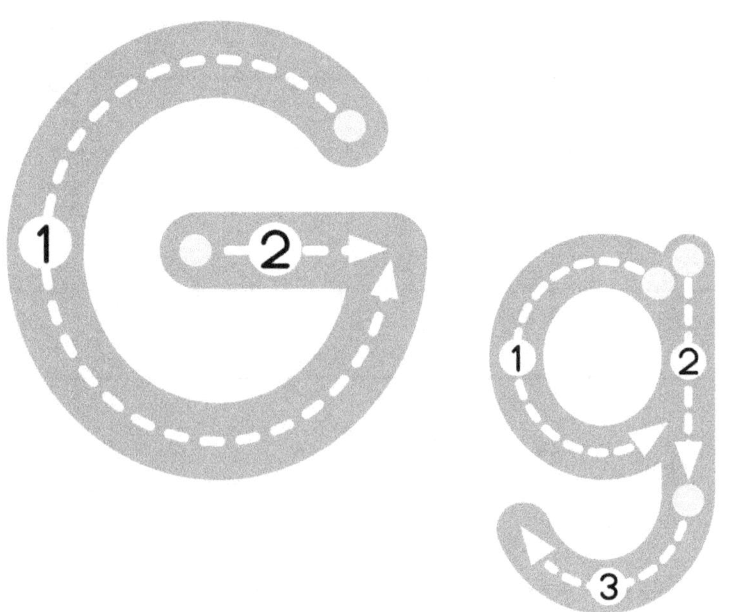

1
2
1
2
3

G is for.........

Goose
Gibbon
Gift
Gorilla
Giraffe
Ghost
Goat
Garbage Truck

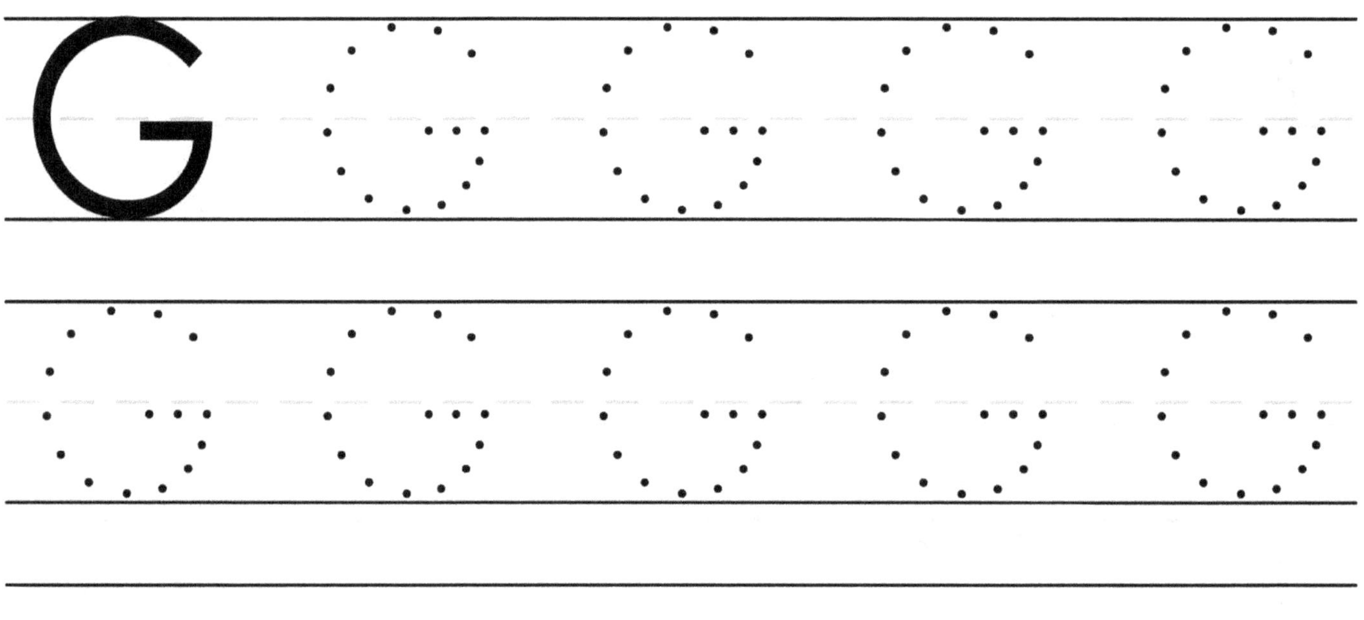

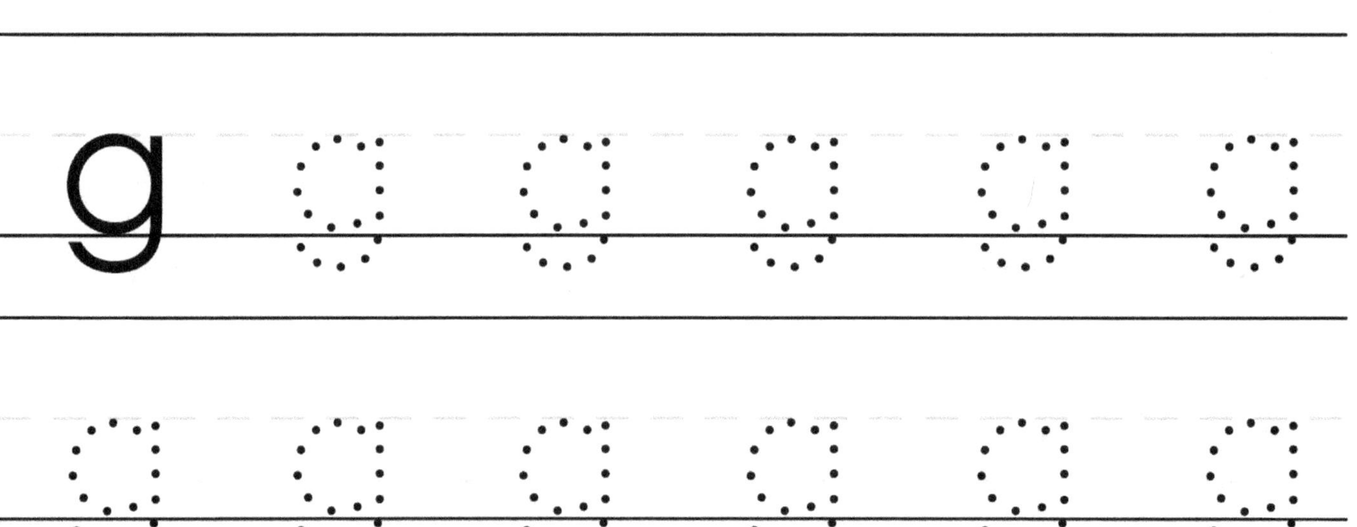

G

G

G

g

1
3
2
1
2

H is for.........

Helicopter
Heart
Horse
House
Hat
Hippo
Hug
Hedgehog

H

h

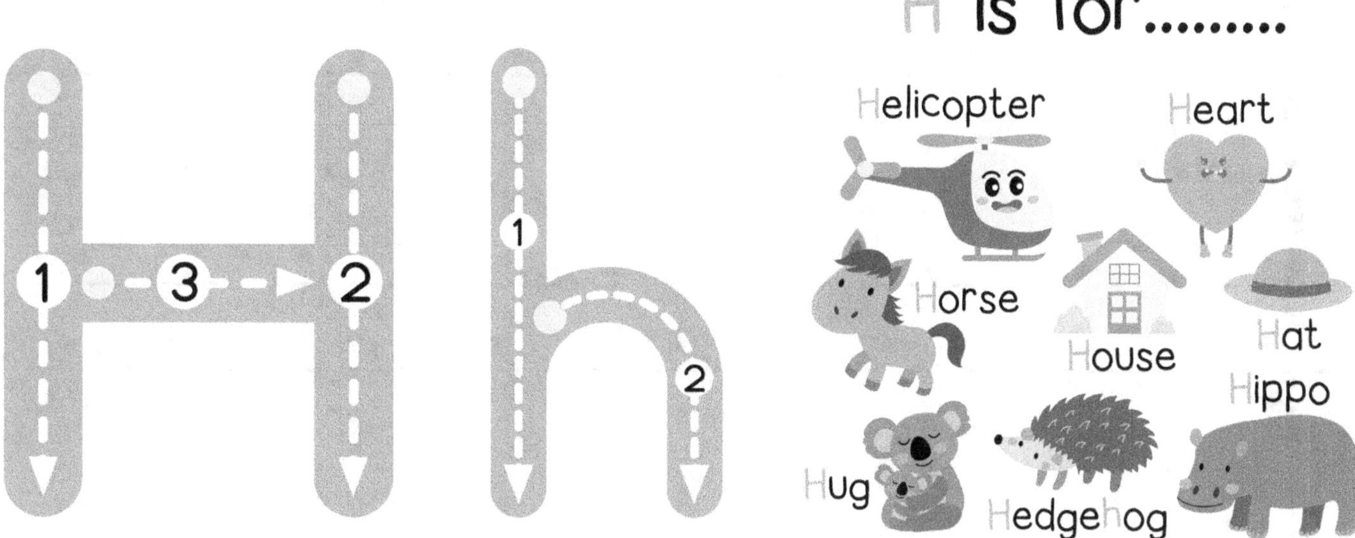

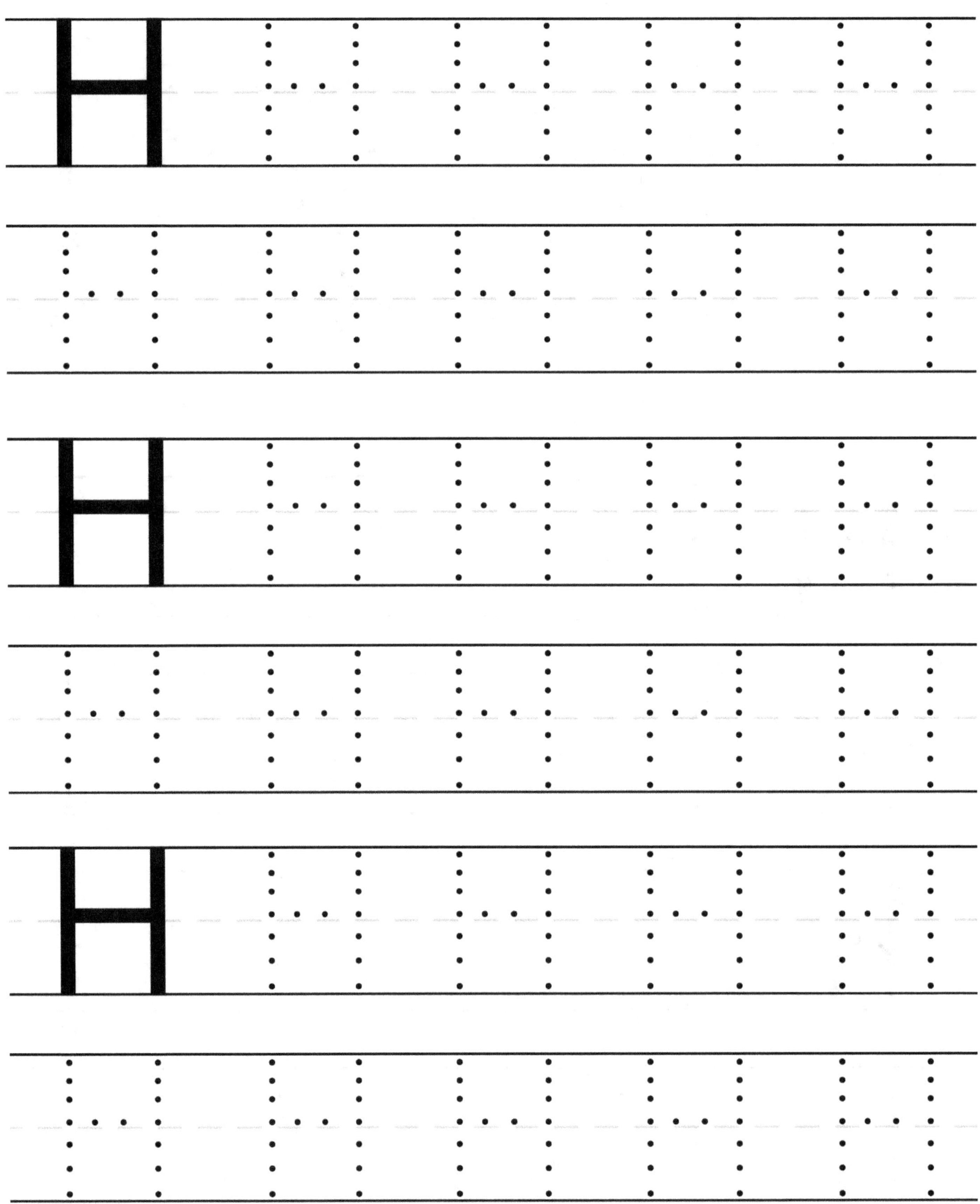

h

h

h

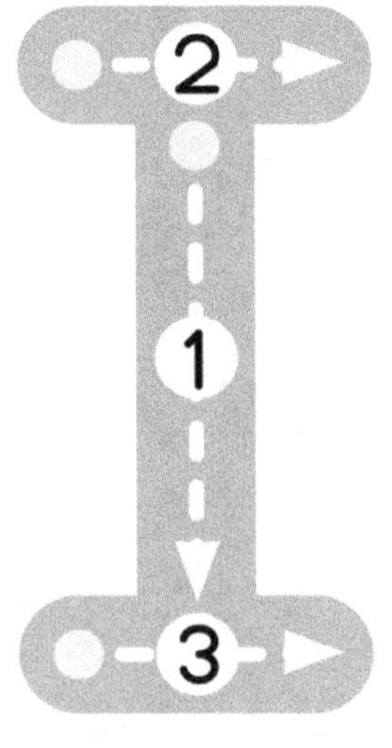

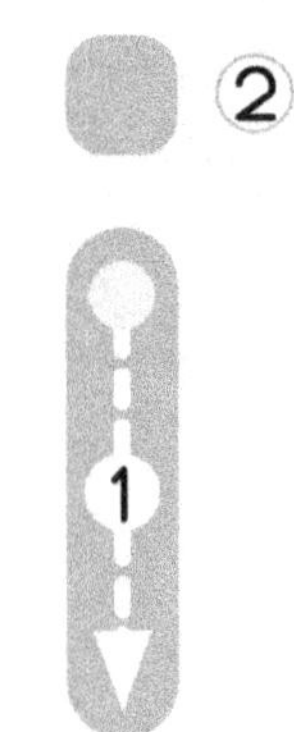

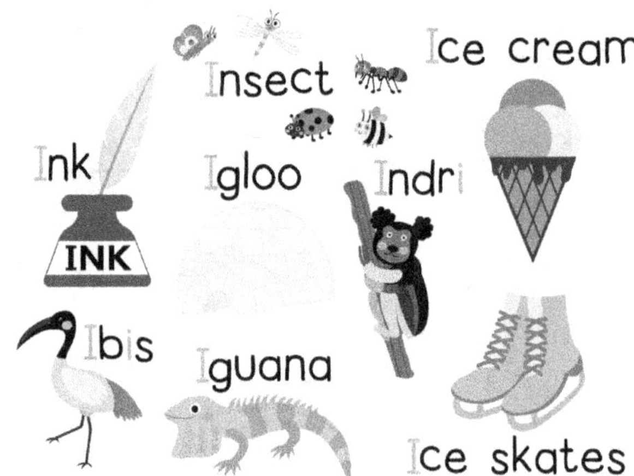

I is for.........

2
1
3

2
1

Insect
Ice cream
Ink
Igloo
Indri
INK
Ibis
Iguana
Ice skates

I

I

i

i

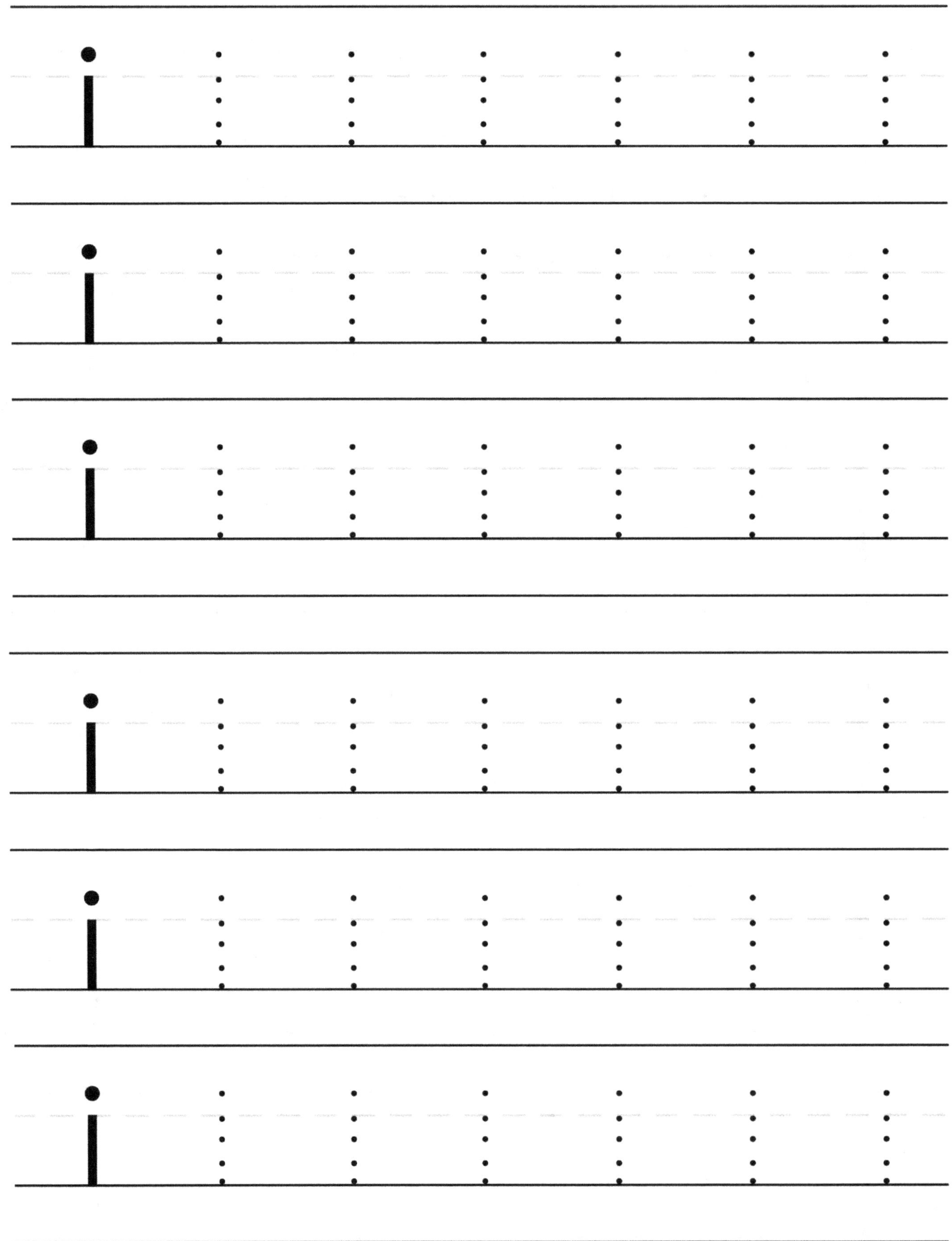

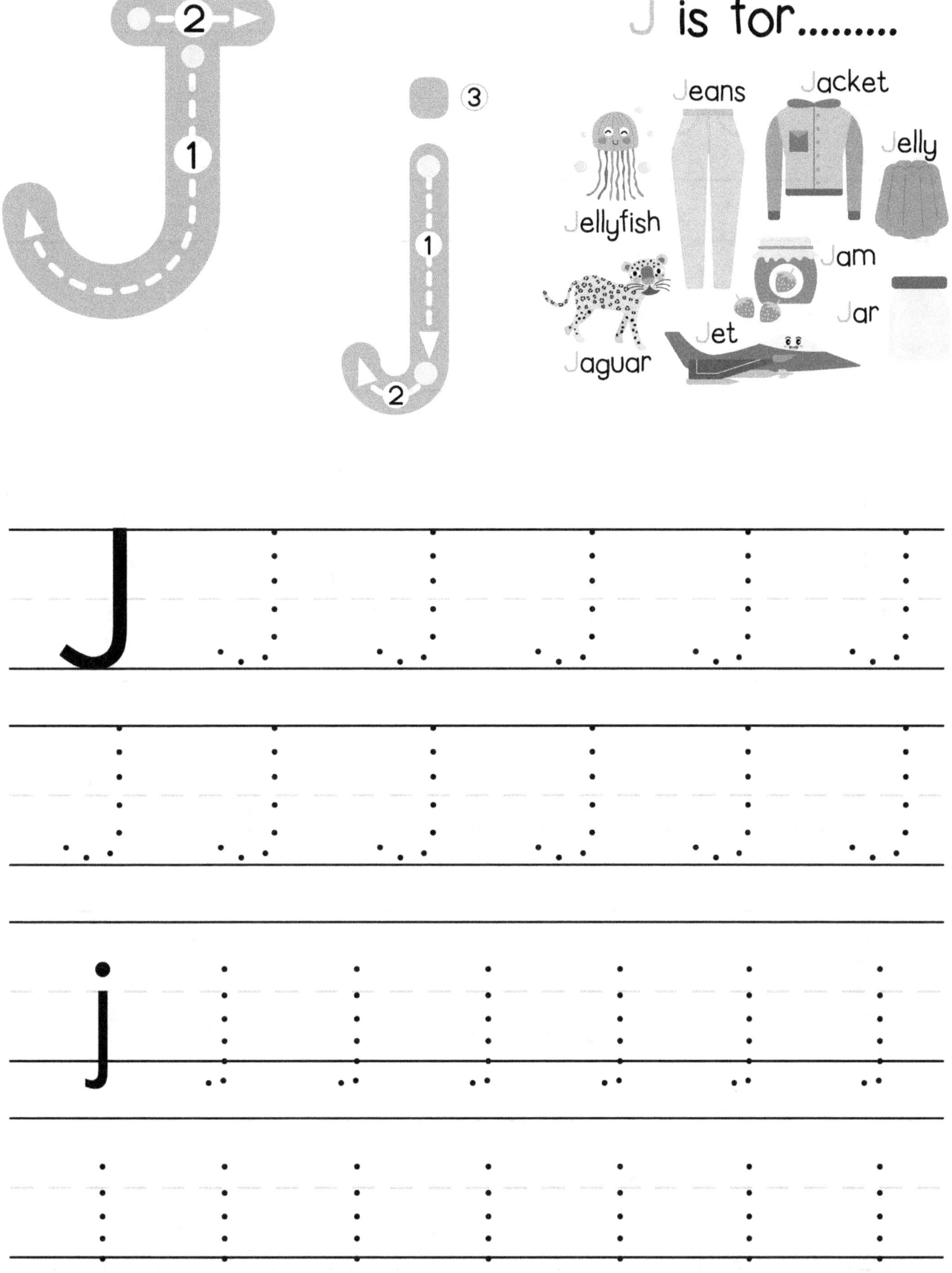

2
1
j
3
1
2
J is for........
Jellyfish
Jeans
Jacket
Jelly
Jam
Jar
Jet
Jaguar
J
j

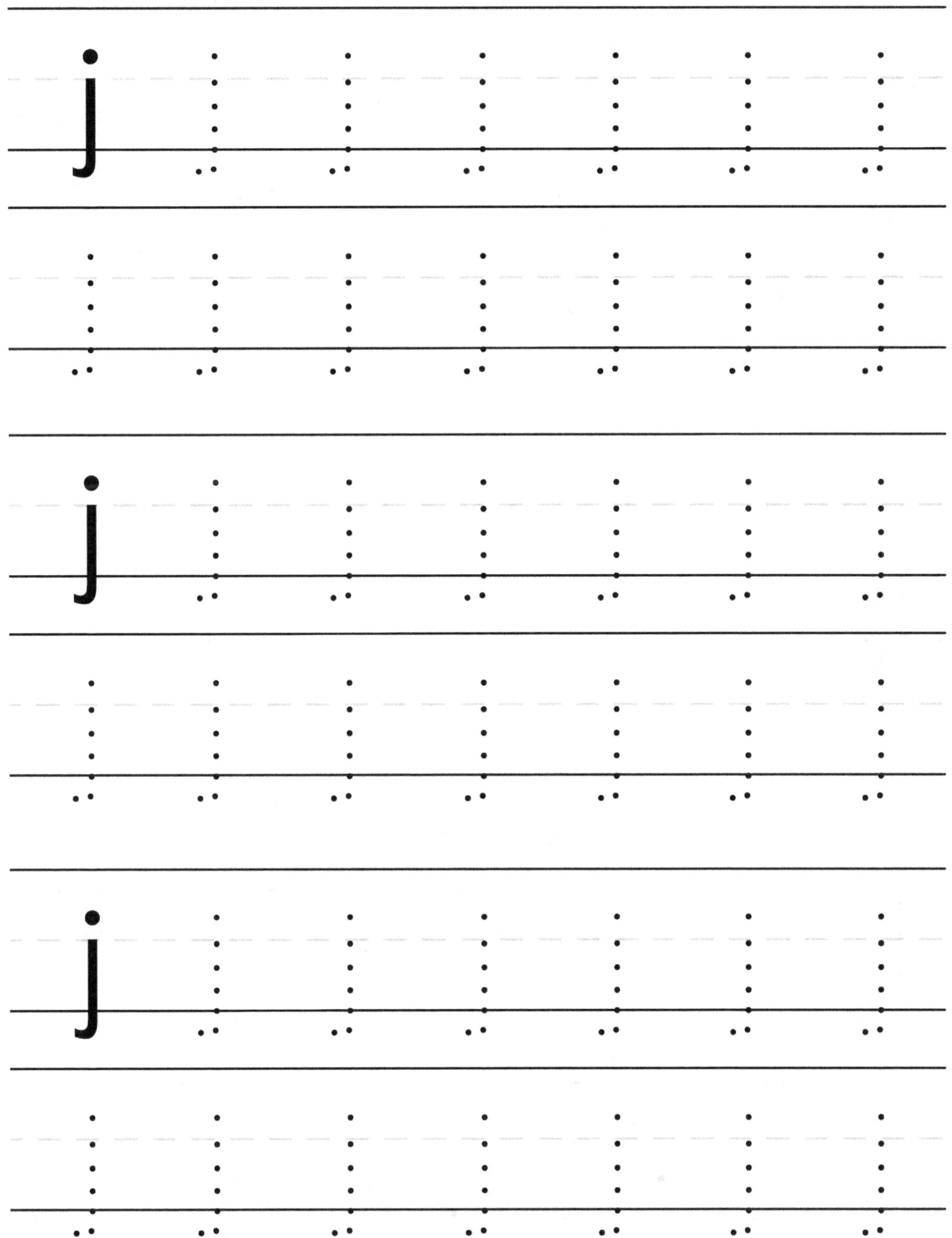

1
2
3
1
2
3

K is for.........

Kiss
Koala
Key
Kite
King
Kiwi
Kayak
Kangaroo

K

k

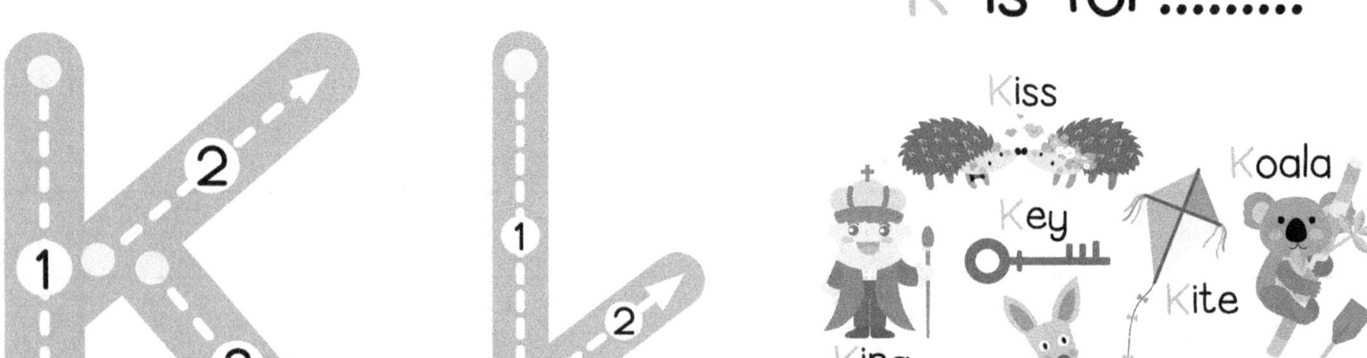

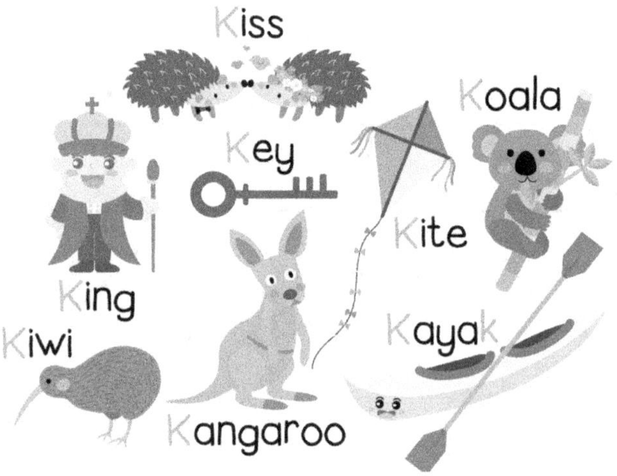

K K K K K

K K K K K

K

K K K K K

K K K K K

K

K K K K K

K K K K K

k k k k k k k

k k k k k k k

k k k k k k k

k k k k k k k

k k k k k k k

k k k k k k k

k k k k k k k

1
2

1

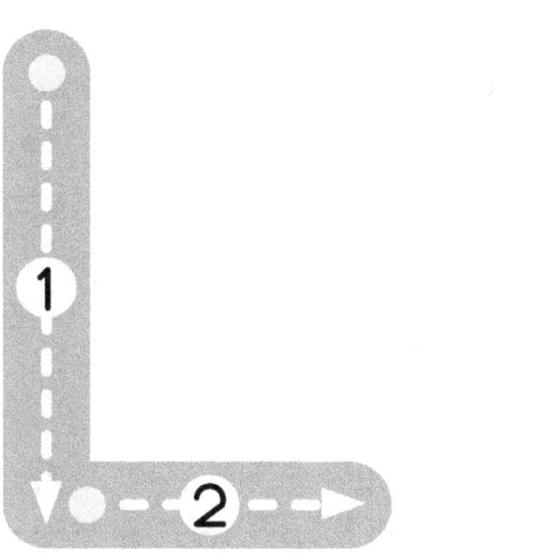

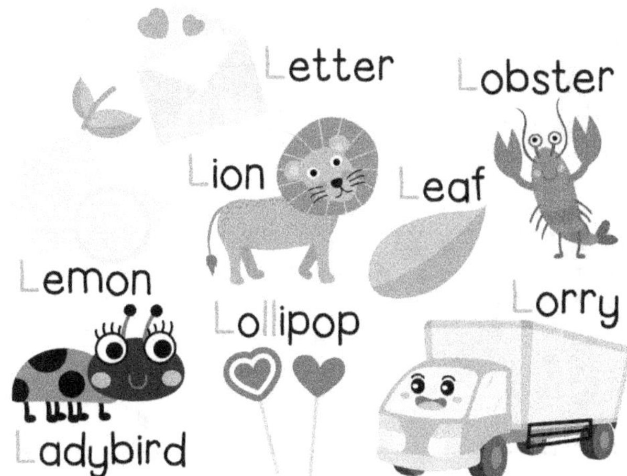

L is for.........

Letter
Lobster
Lion
Leaf
Lemon
Lollipop
Lorry
Ladybird

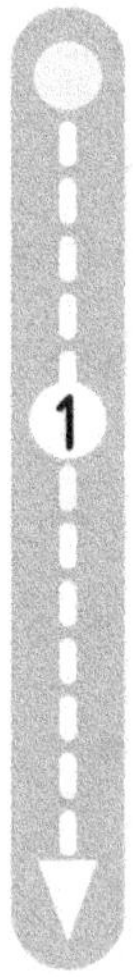

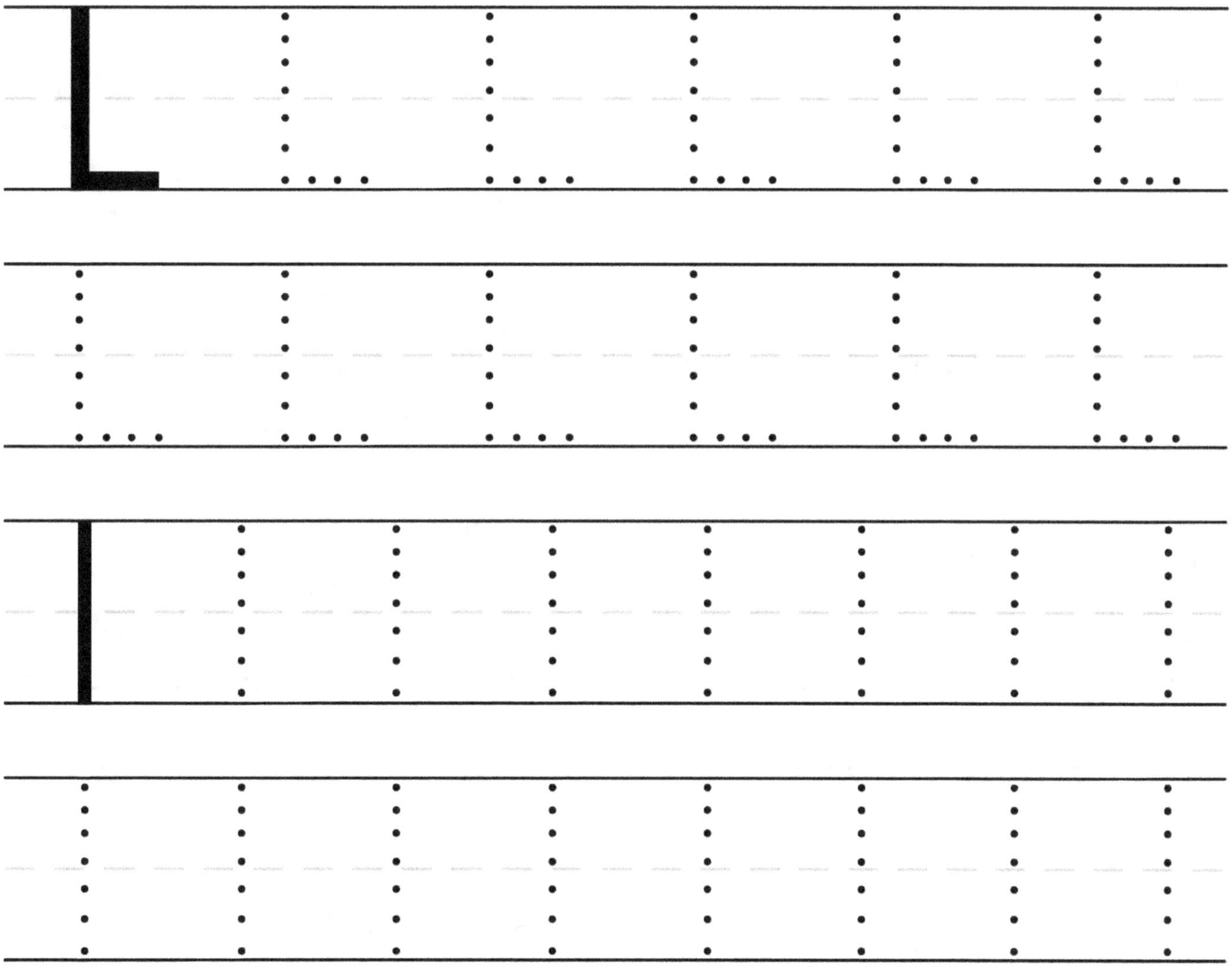

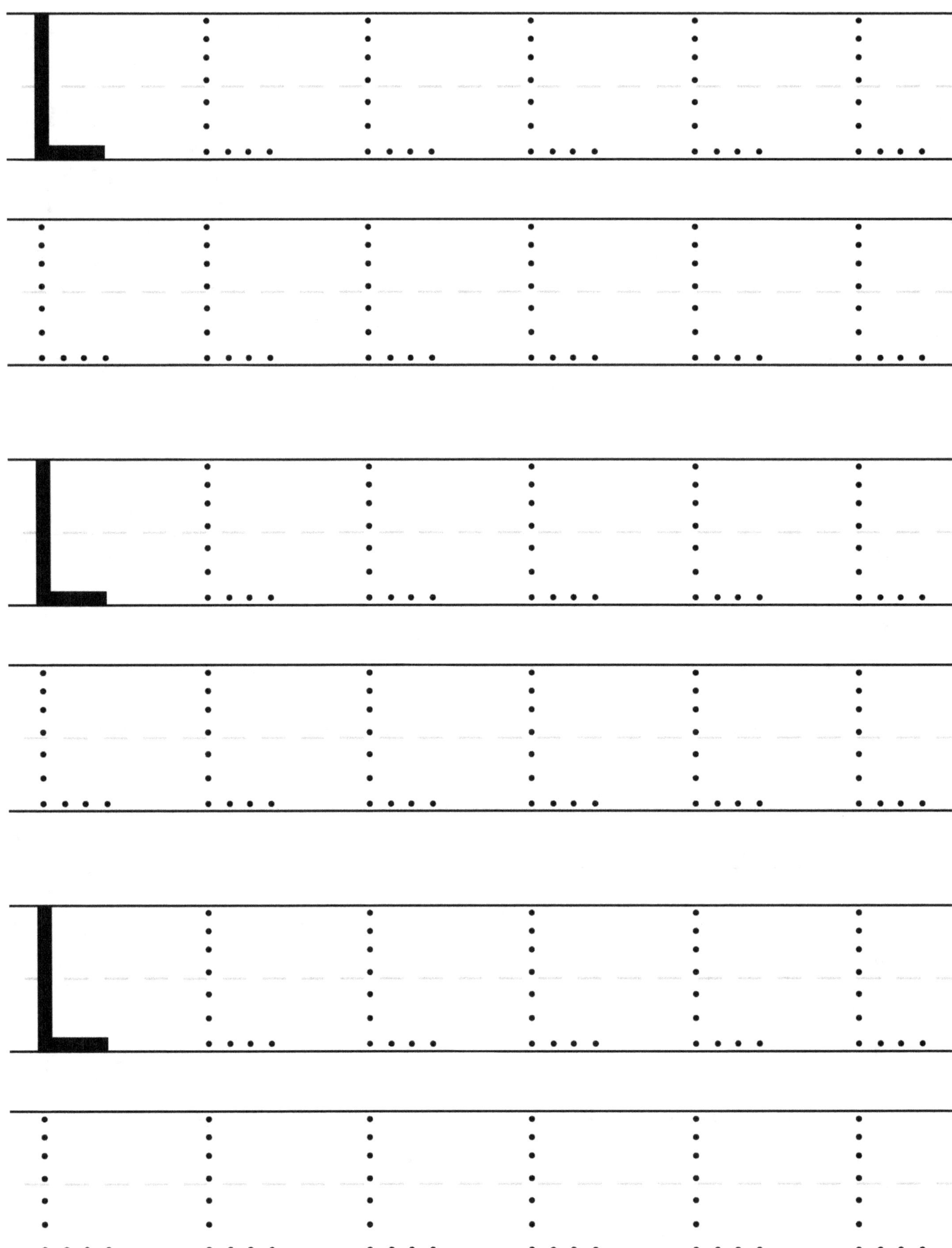

I

I

I

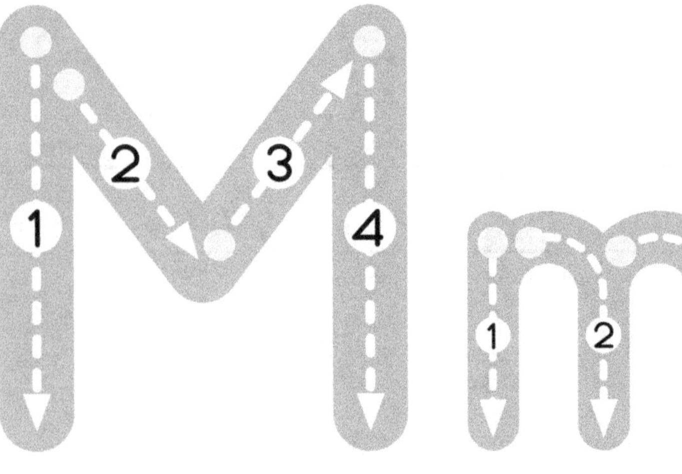

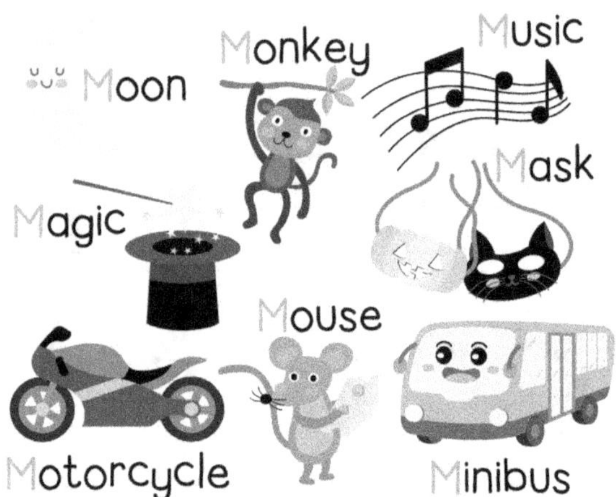

M is for.........

Moon
Monkey
Music
Mask
Magic
Mouse
Motorcycle
Minibus

M

m

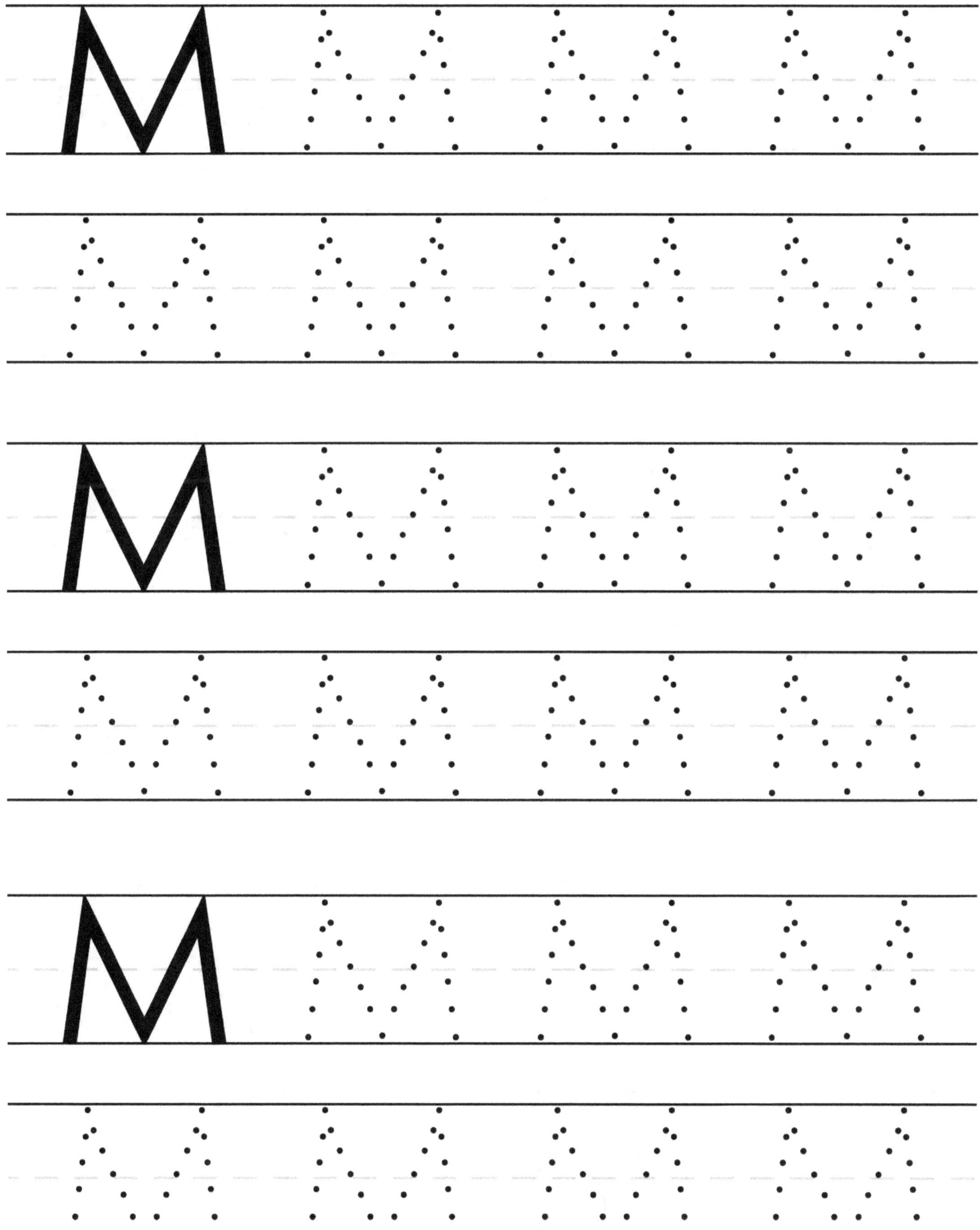

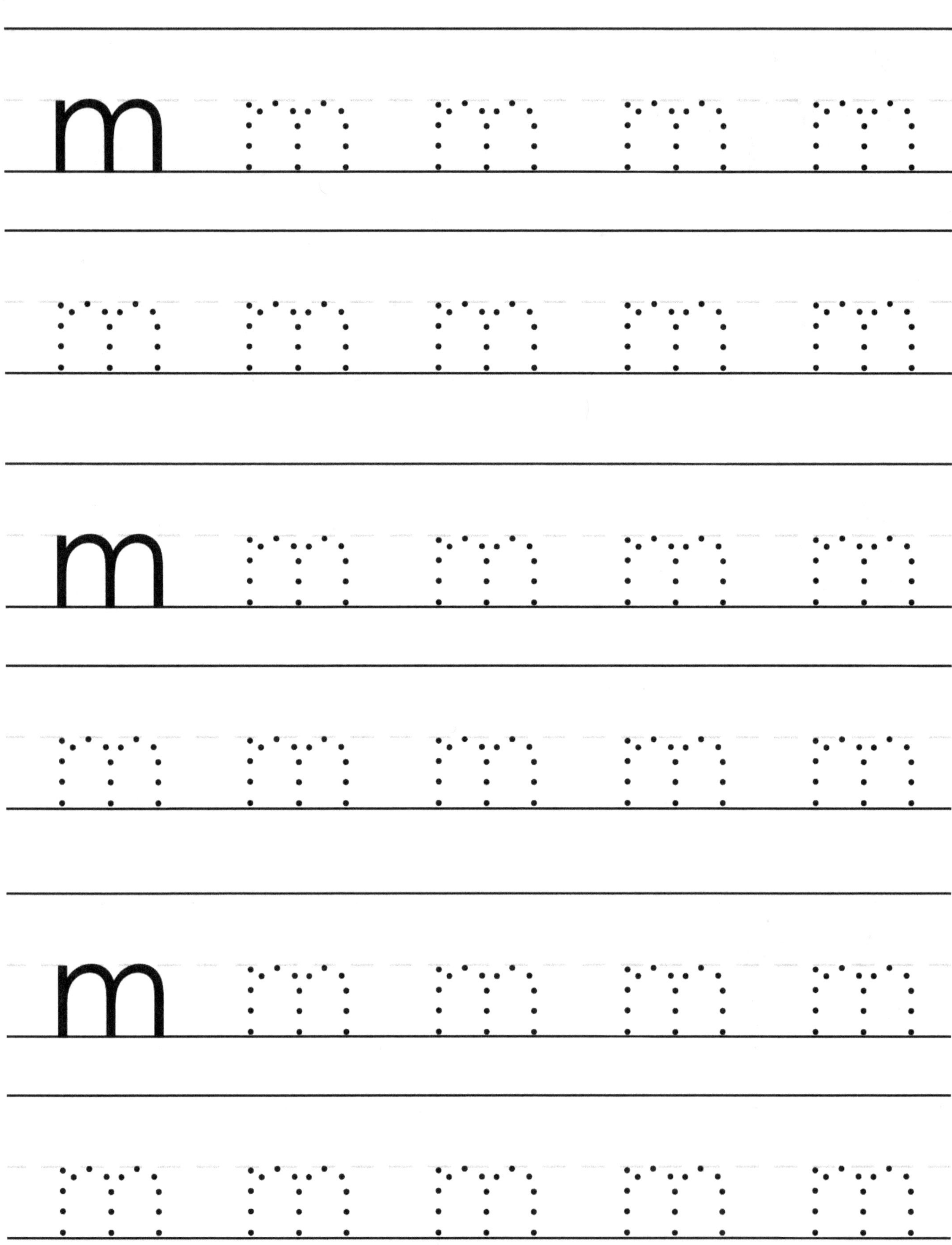

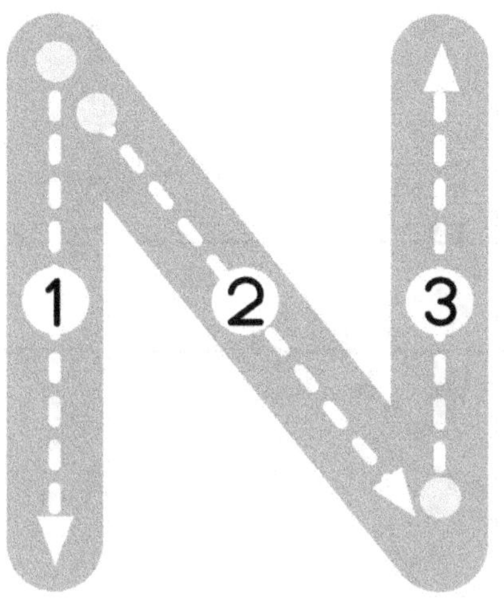

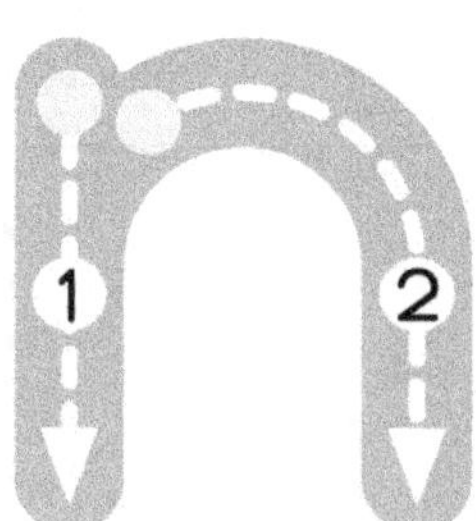

N is for.........
Nightingale
Nest
Ninja
Needle
Narwhal
Night
Necktie
Notebook

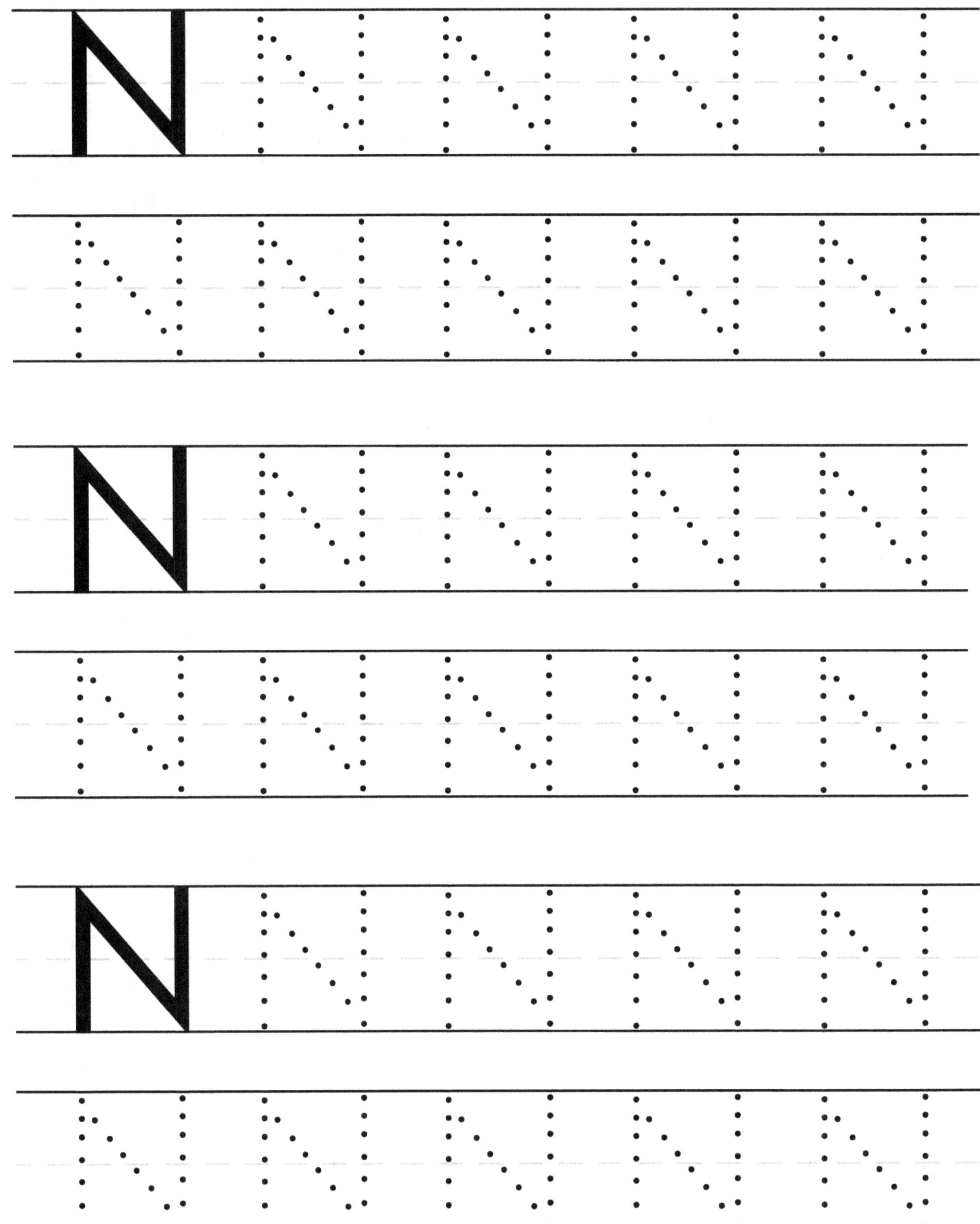

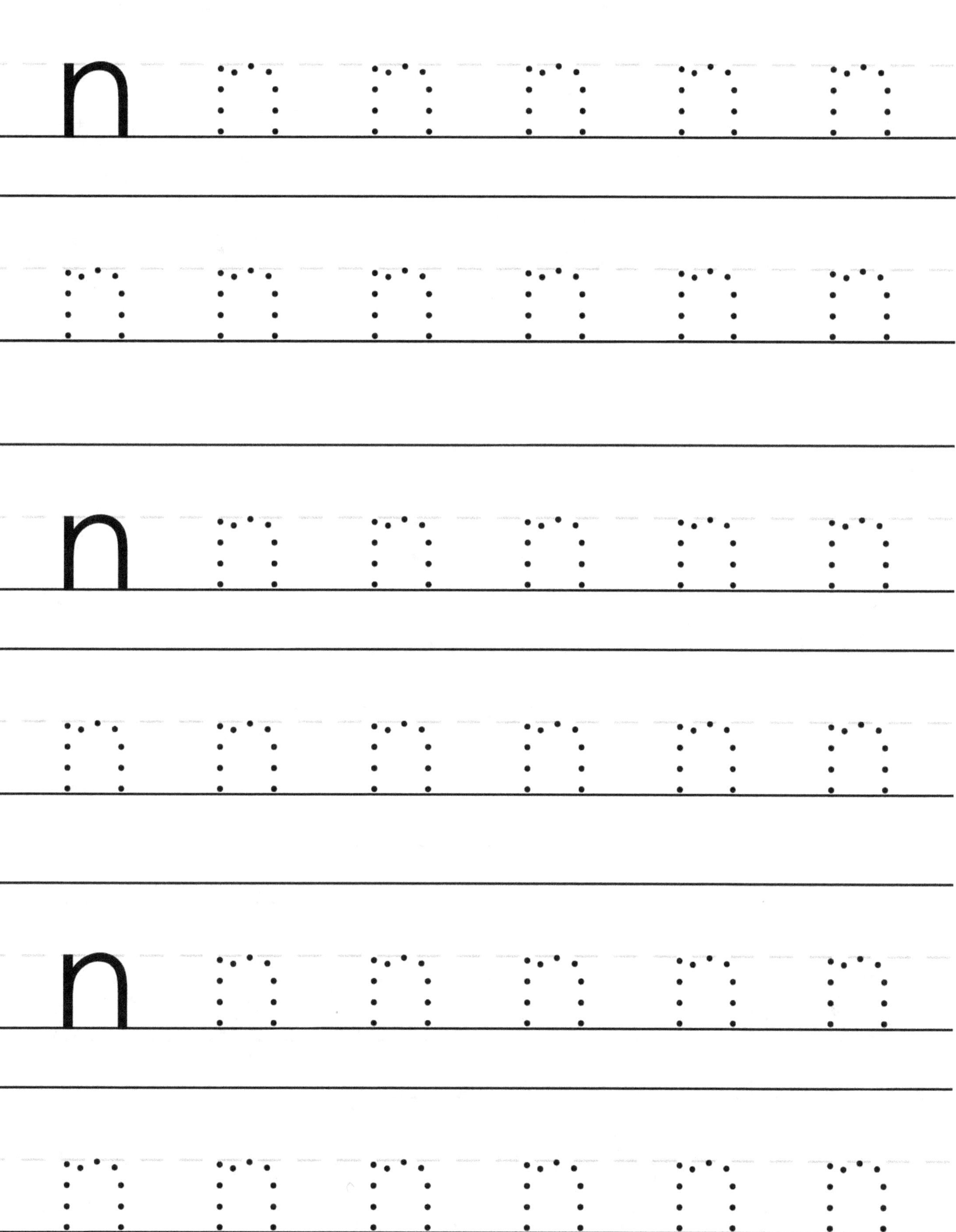

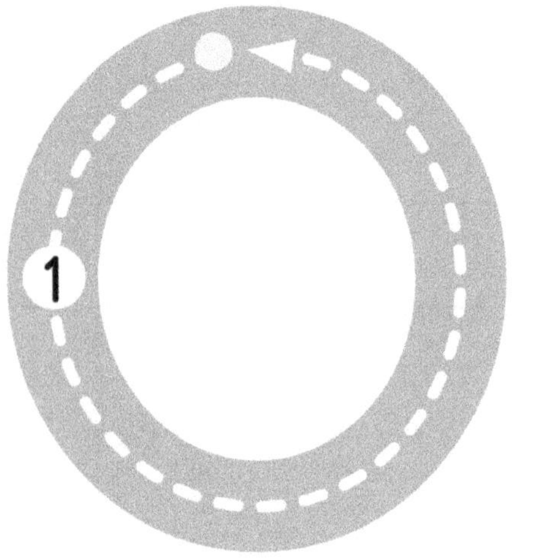

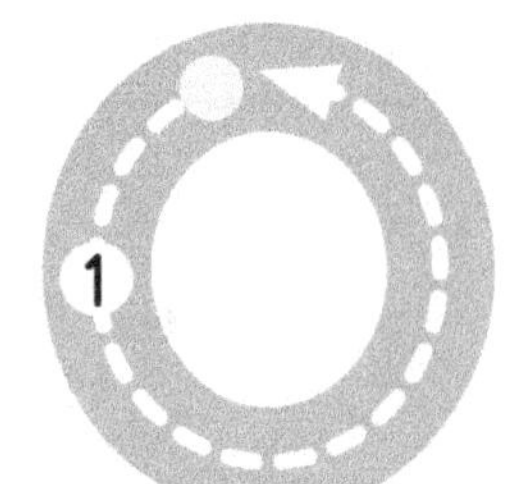

O is for.........
Owl
Octopus
Oyster
Orangutan
Ostrich
Orange
OIL
Oval
Oil Tanker Truck

O

O

O

O o o o o o o

o o o o o o o

O o o o o o o

o o o o o o o

O o o o o o o

o o o o o o o

P   P P P P P P

P   P P P P P P

p   p p p p p p

p   p p p p p p

P P P P P P P
P P P P P P
P P P P P P P
P P P P P P
P P P P P P P
P P P P P P

p p p p p p p p p

p p p p p p p

p p p p p p p p

p p p p p p p

p p p p p p p p

p p p p p p p p

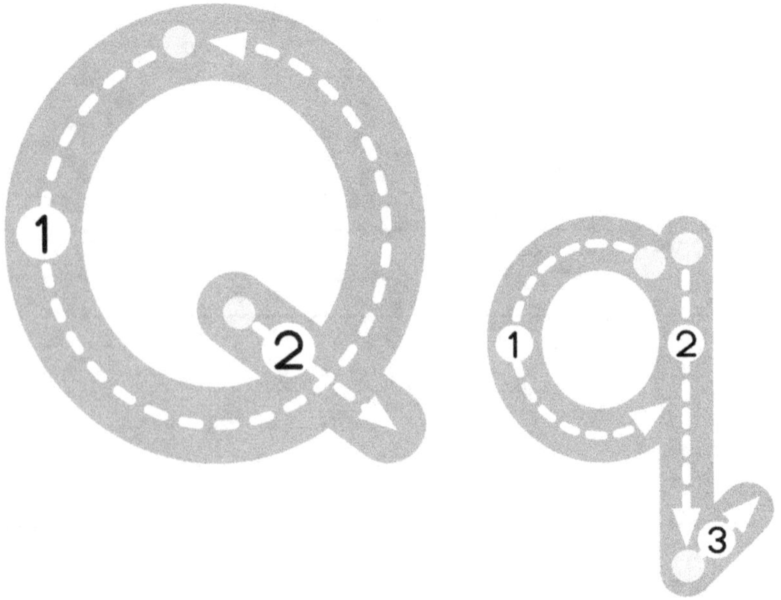

Q q is for........

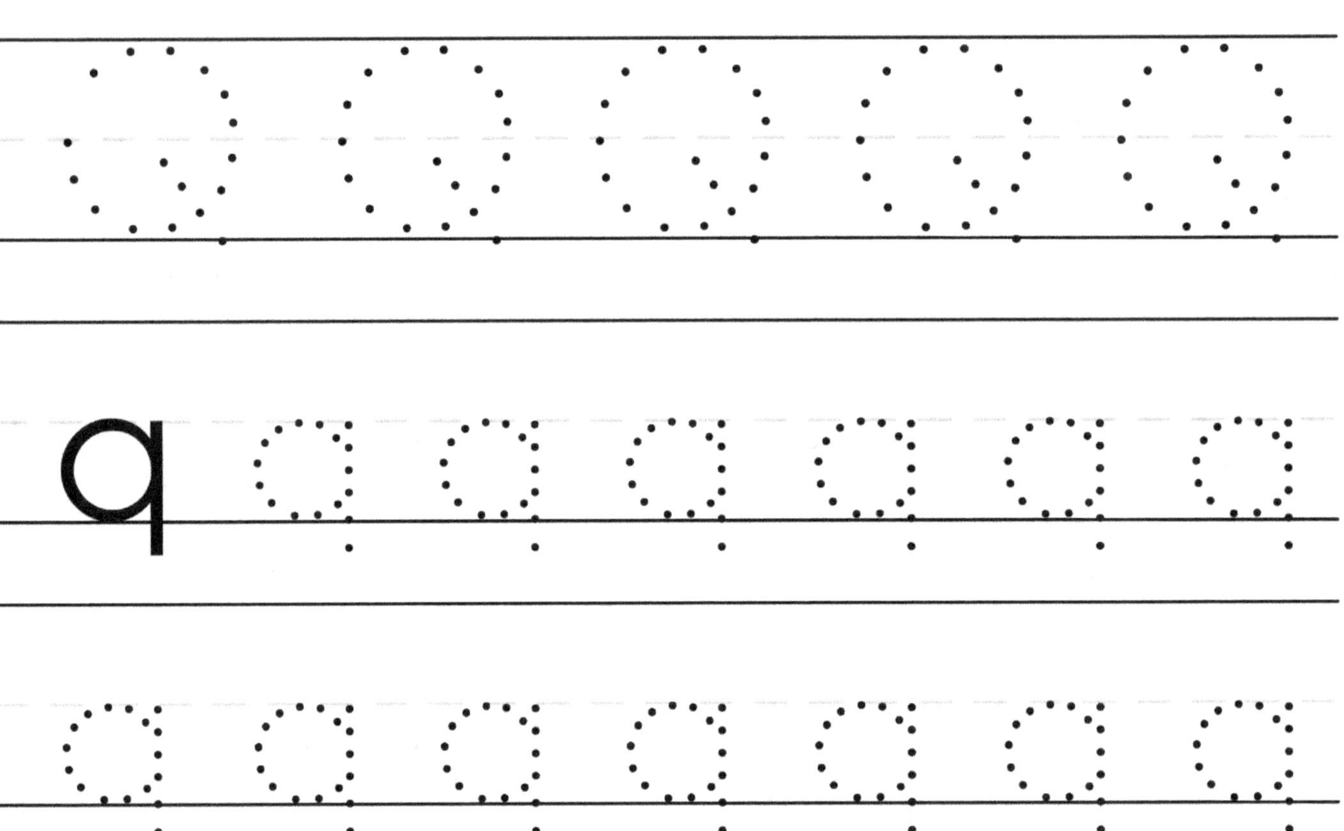

Q

q

Q

q a a a a a a

a a a a a a a

q a a a a a a

q a a a a a a

a a a a a a a

q a a a a a a

1
2
3

2
1

R is for.........

Rocket
Rainbow
Raccoon
Rose
Ring
Robot
Rabbit
Raft
Rectangle

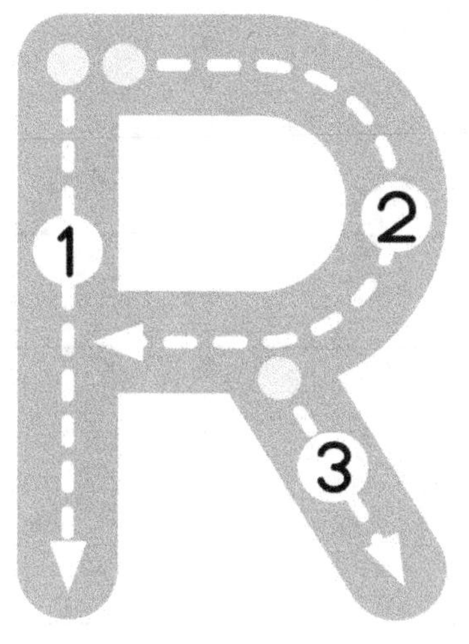

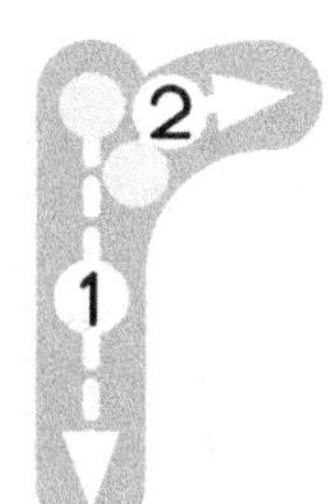

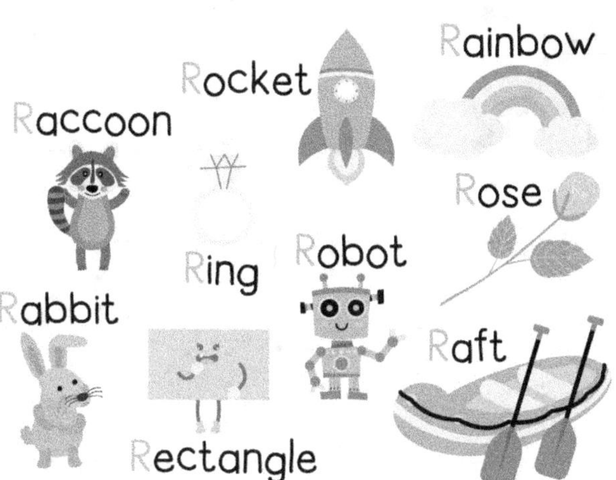

R

r

R

R

R

r

S is for........

Sun
Star
Submarine
Shark
Sweet
Snail
Spider
Square
Snowflake
Seaplane

S

s

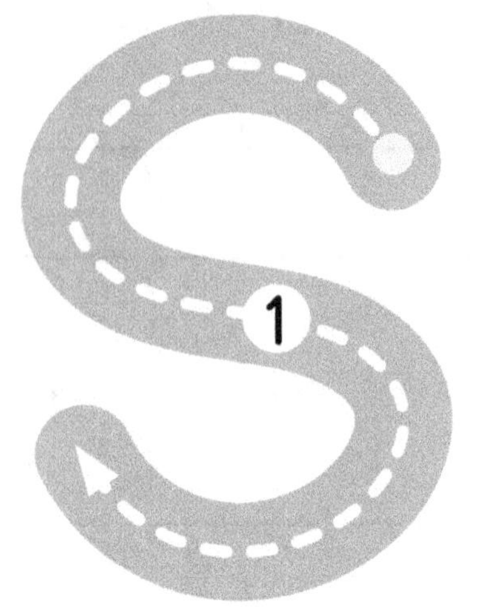

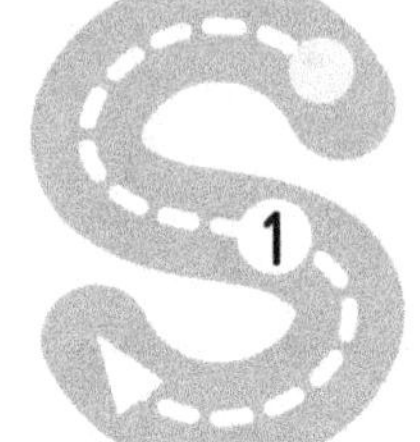

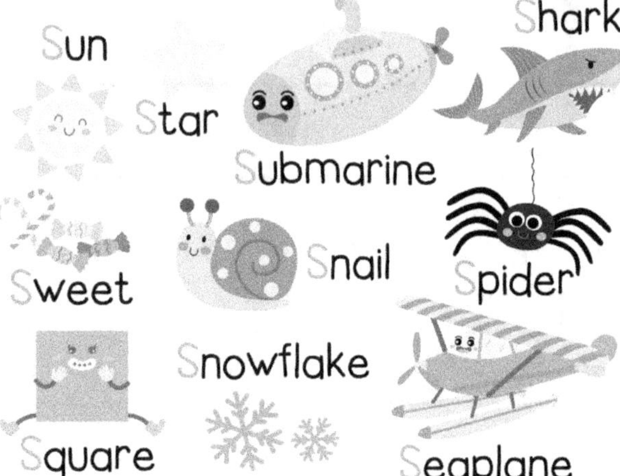

S

S

S

S

2
1
1
3
2
T is for.........
Turtle
Toucan
Train
Taxi
Tree
Truck
Triangle
Tiger
Tricycle

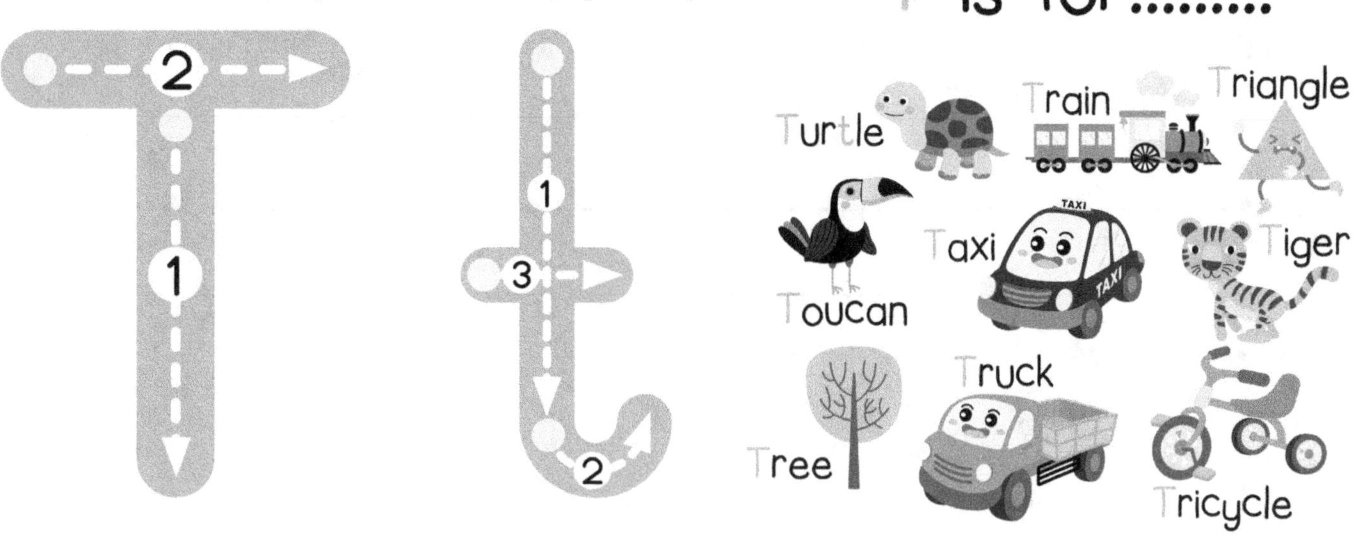

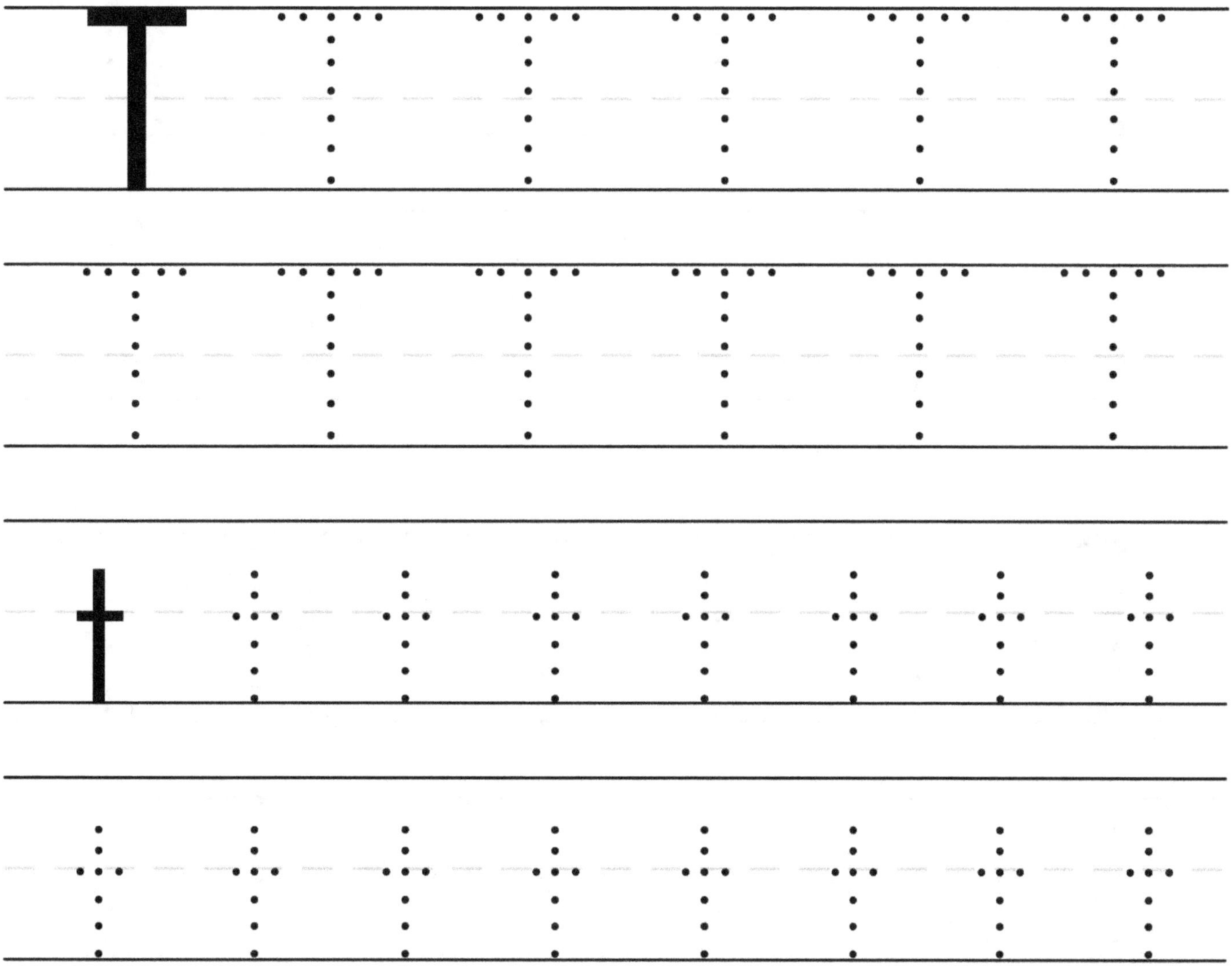

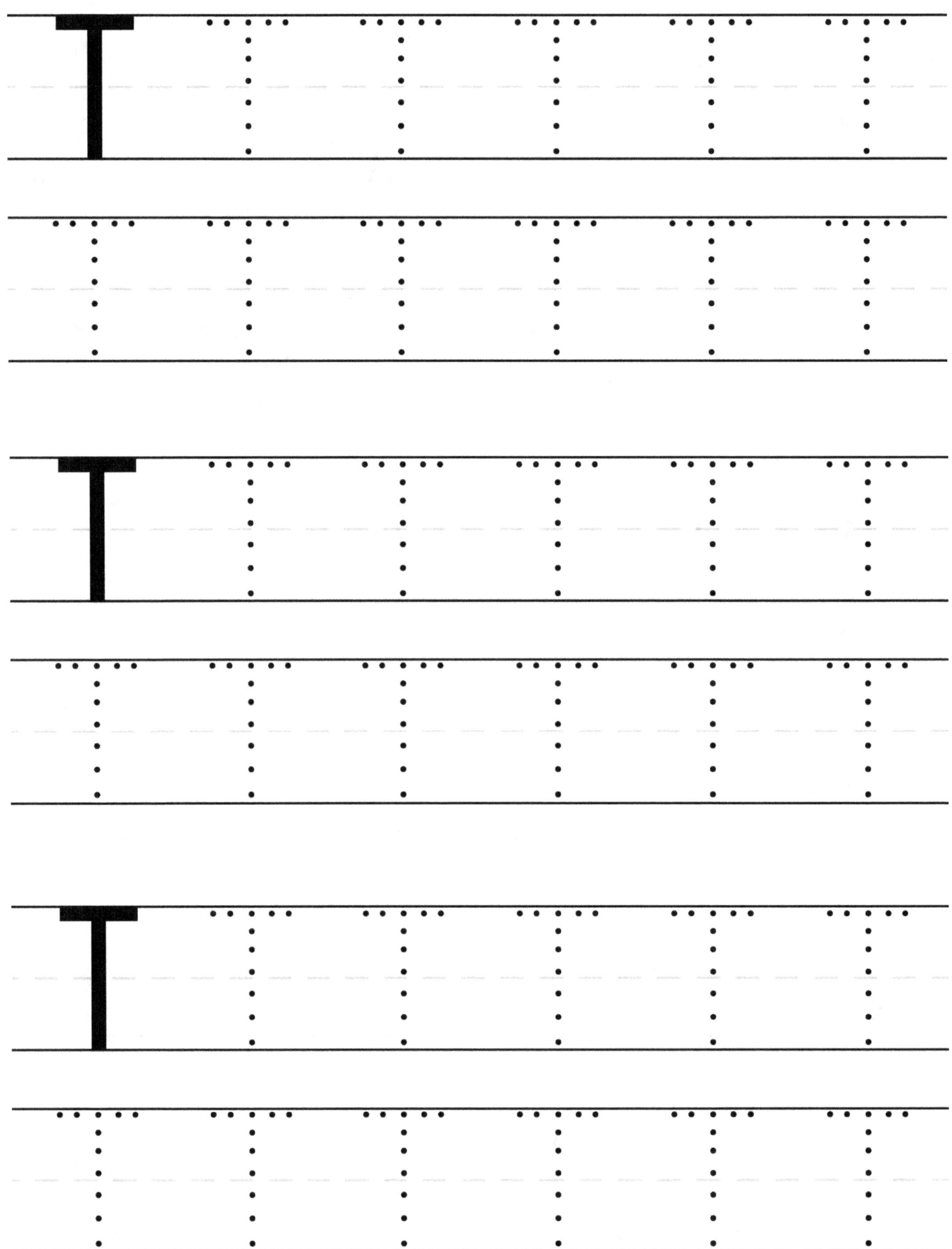

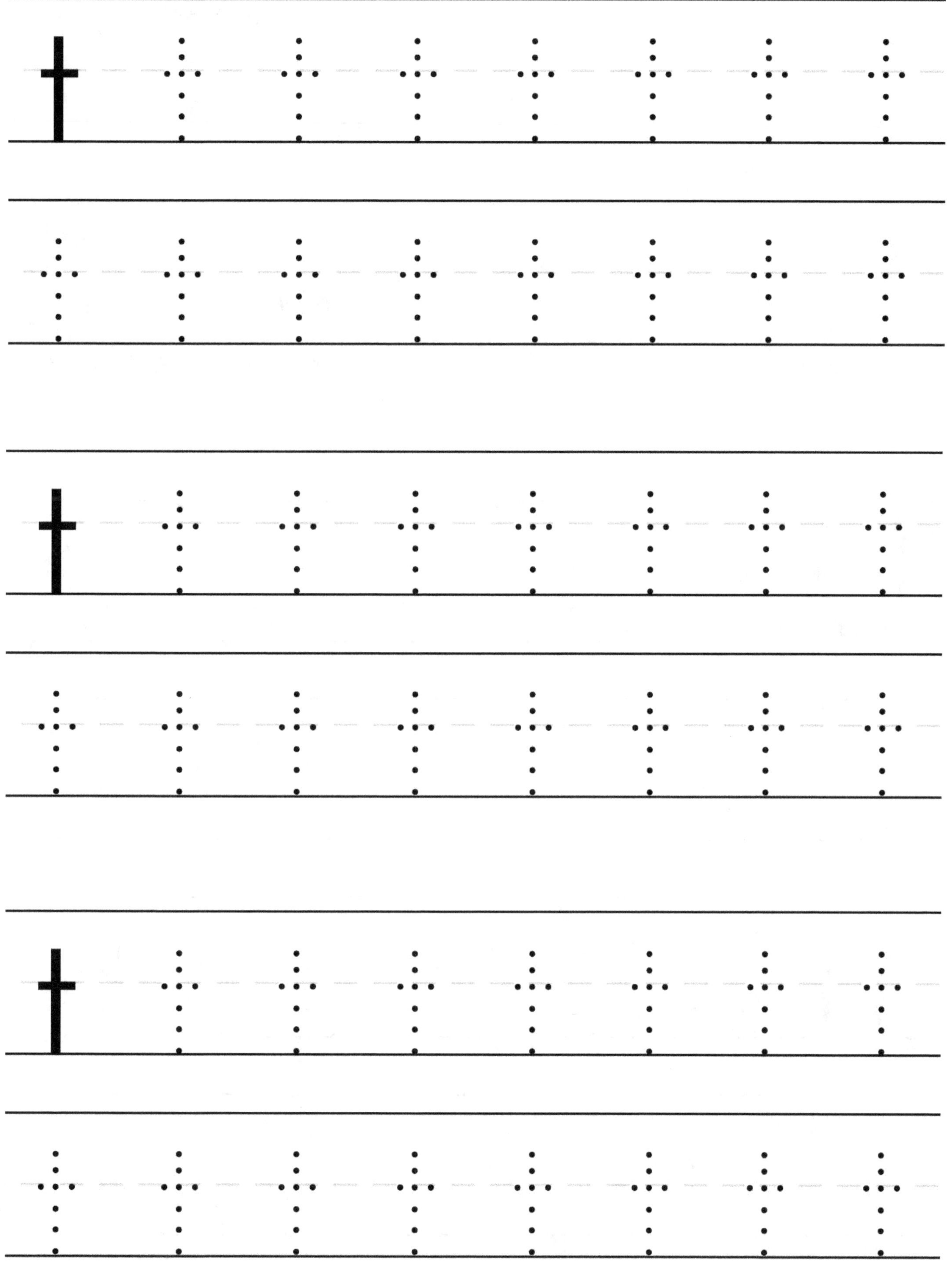

U is for.........

Umbrella
Unicorn
Unicycle
Urchin
Unhappy
UFO

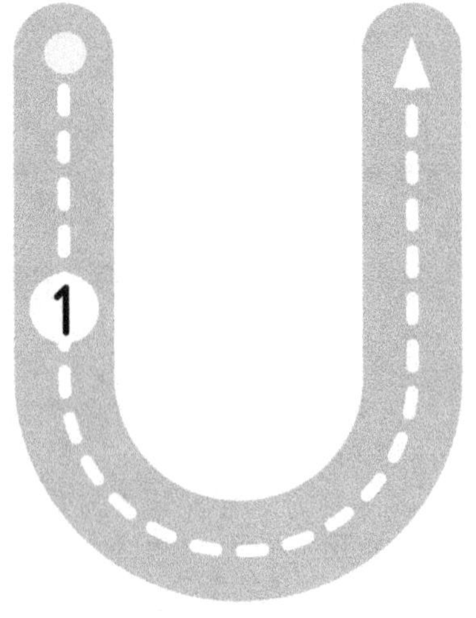

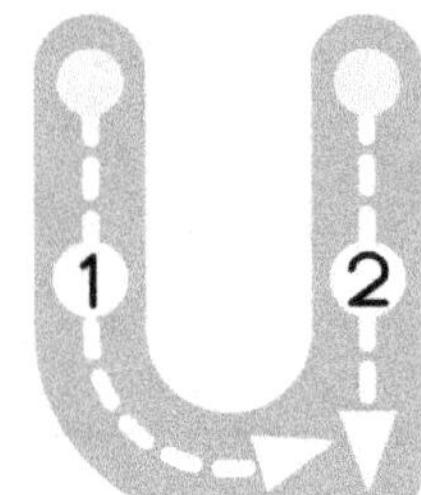

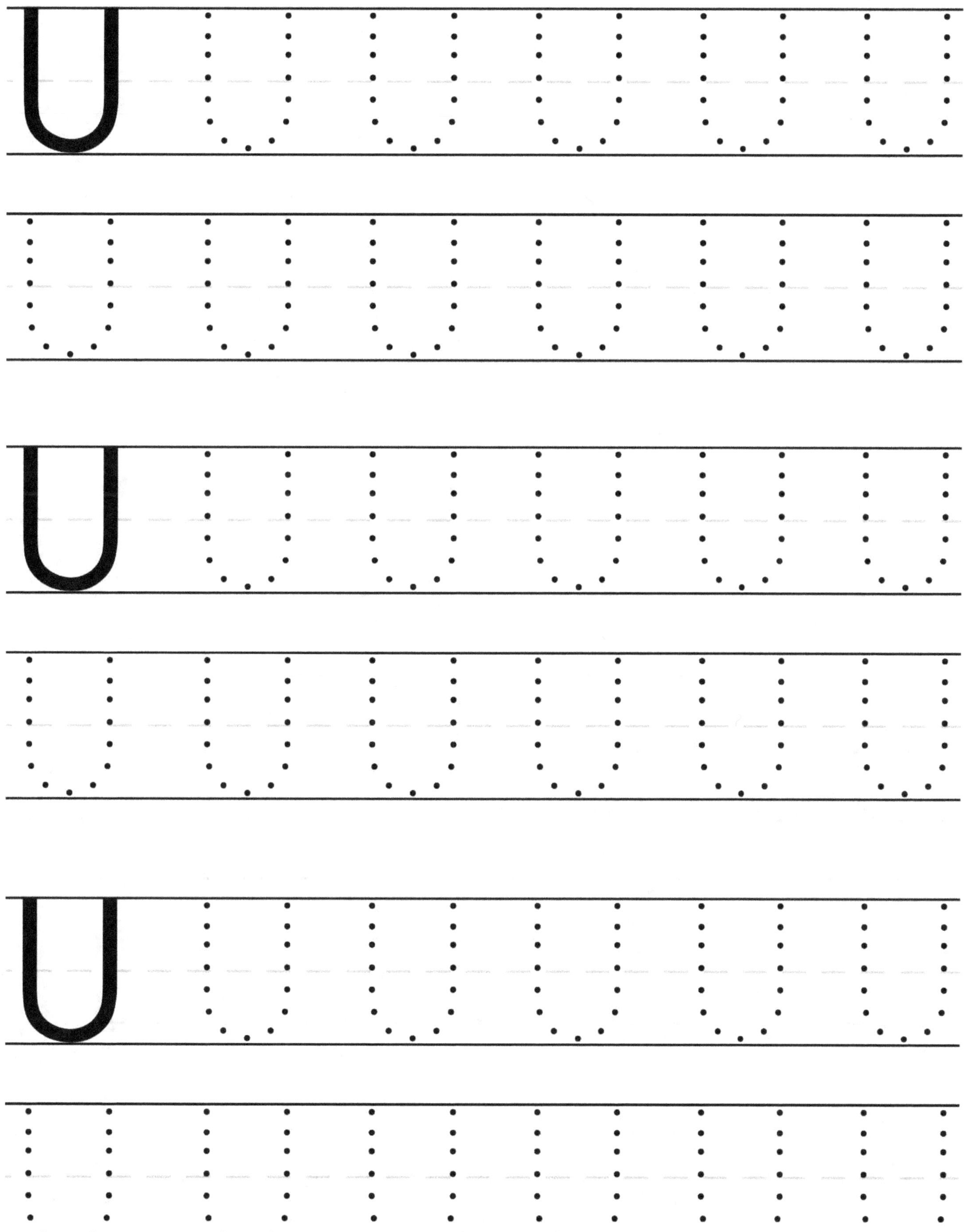

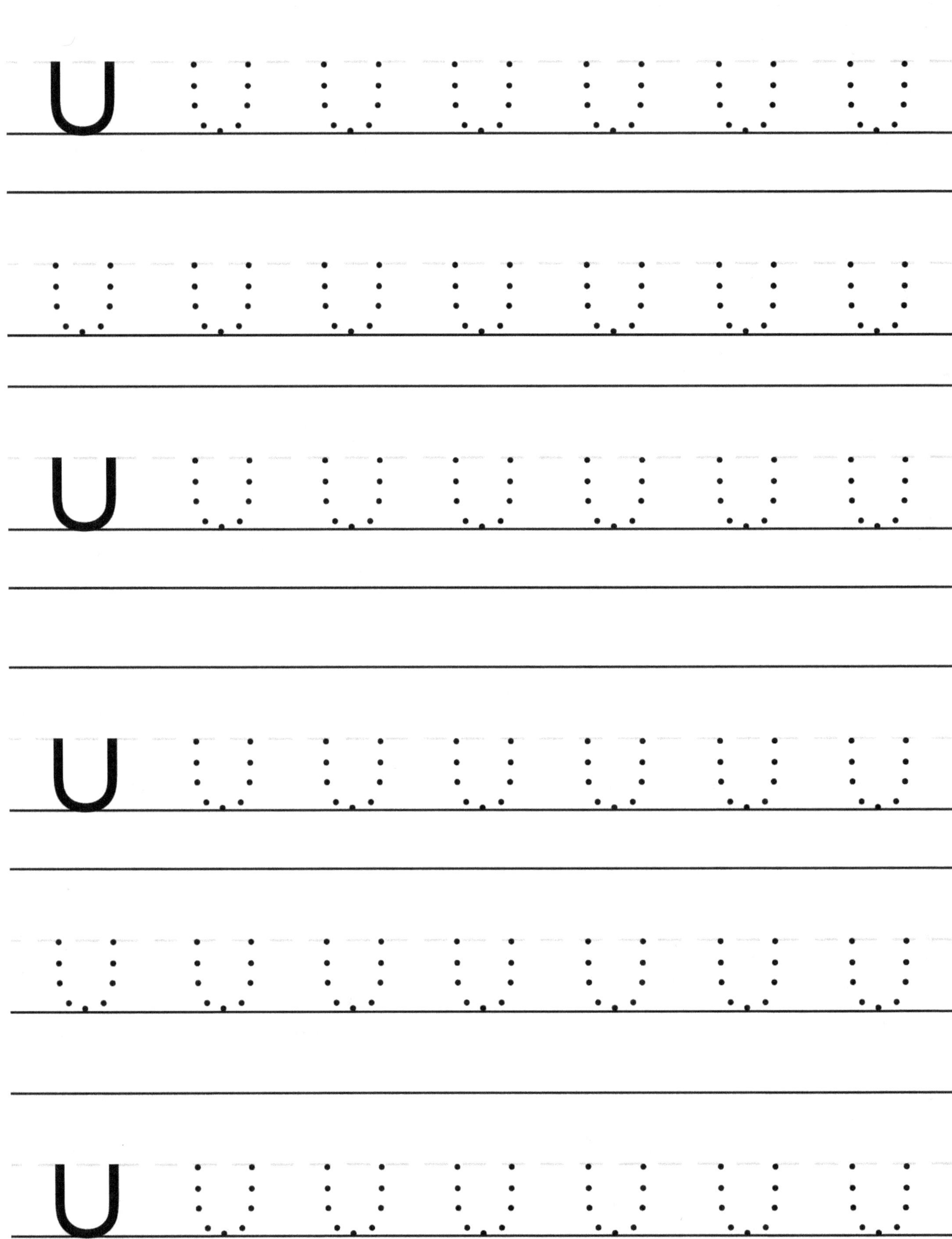

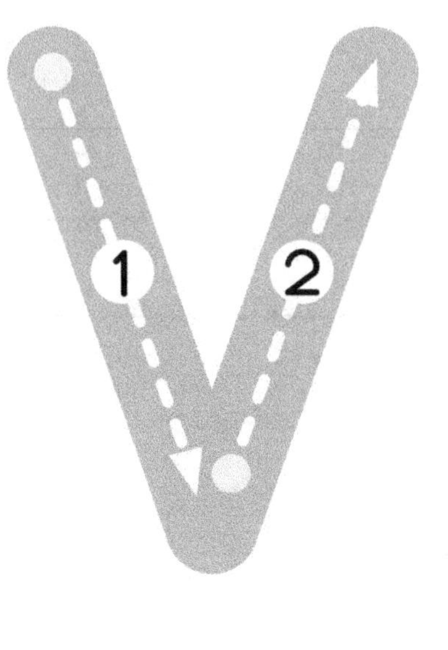
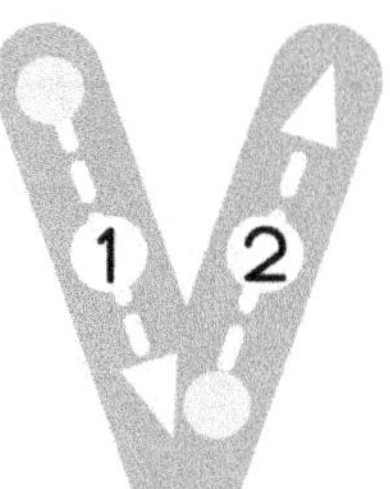

V is for.........
Vase
Volcano
Violin
Vulture
Vampire
Van

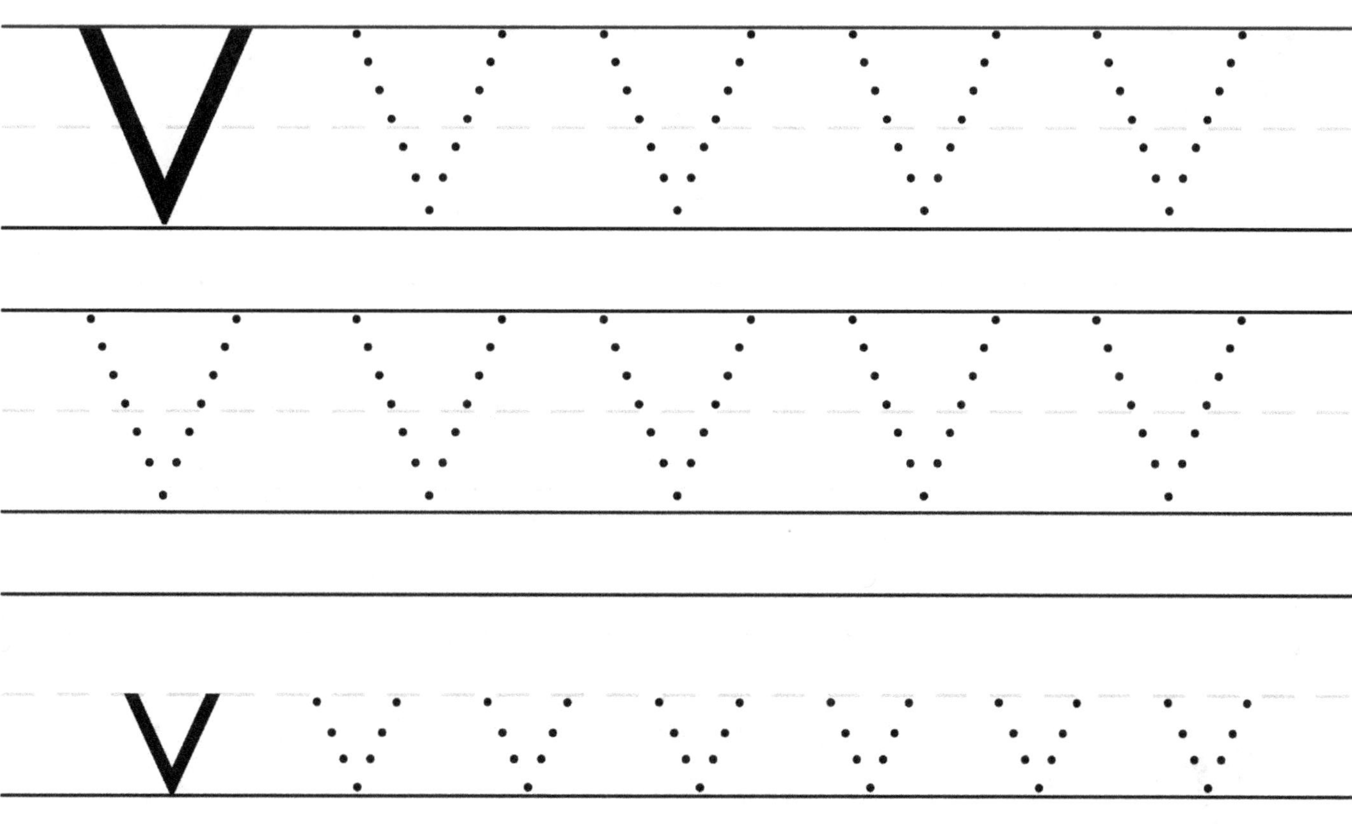

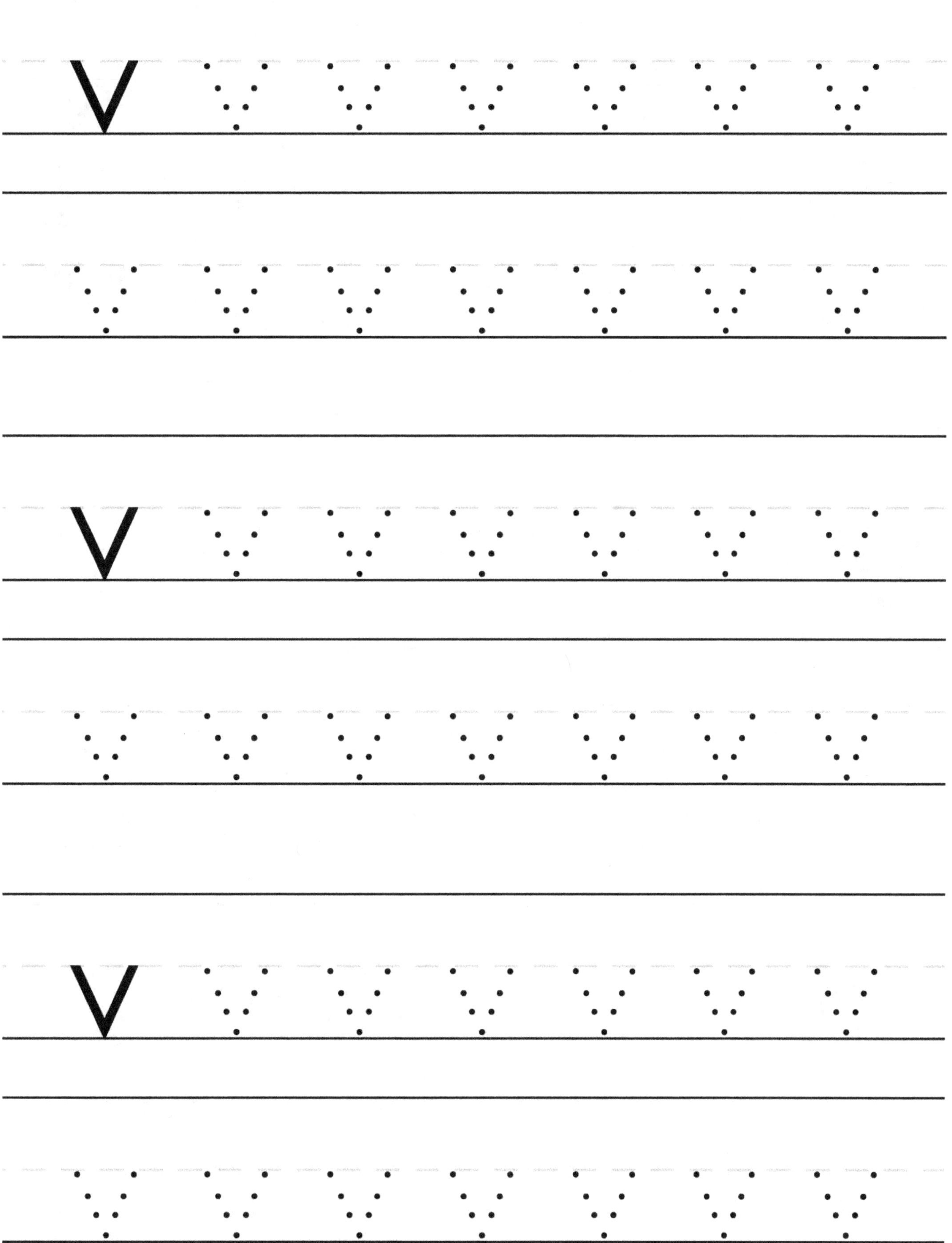

1
2
3
4
1
2
3
4

W is for.........

Web
Wreath
Watermelon
Whale
Warthog
Witch
Wolf
Worm
Wagon

W

w

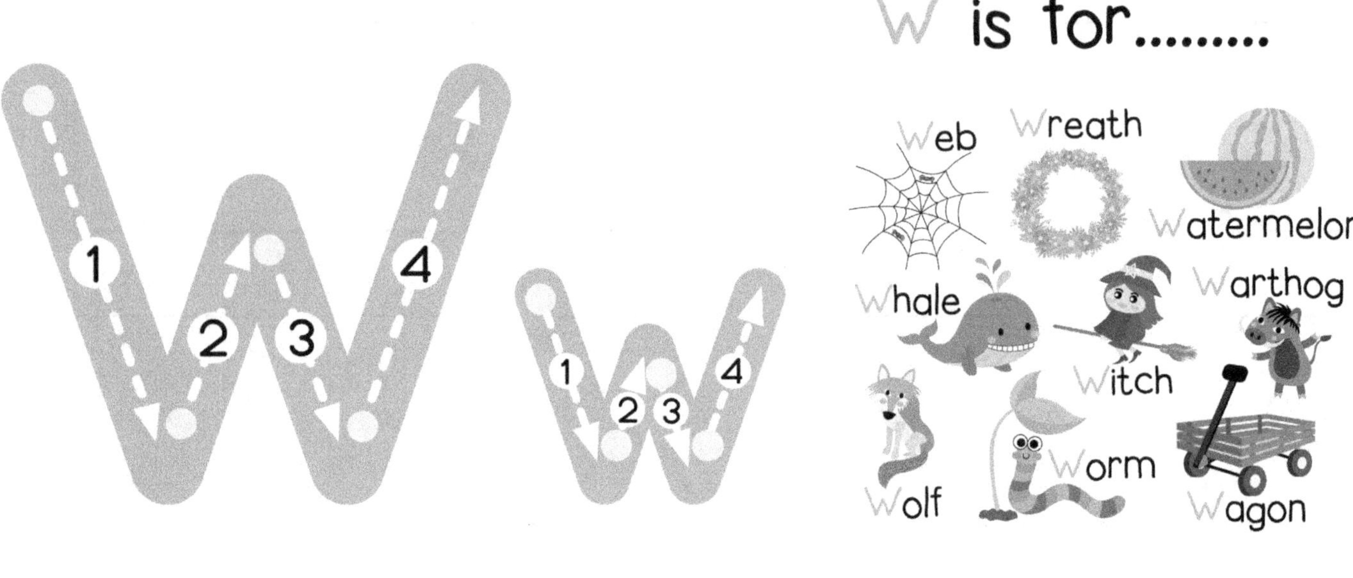

W W W W W W

W W W W W W

W W W W W W

W

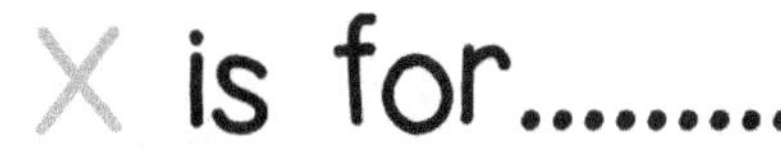

1
2

1
2

X is for.........

Xylophone
X-ray
Xerus
Xmas
Xantus
X-ray Fish
Xmas Sleigh

X

x

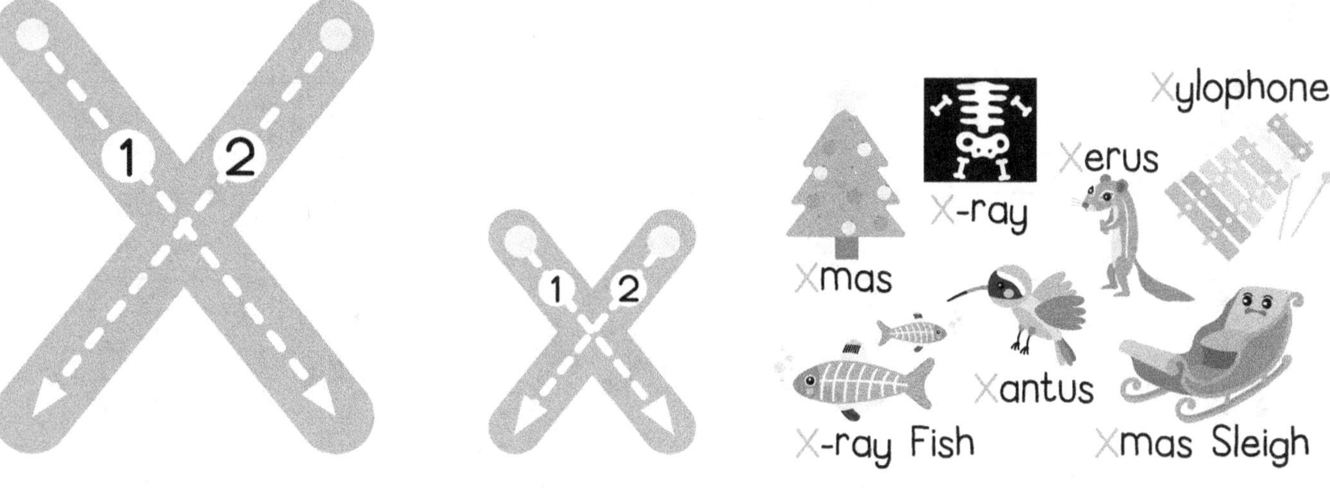

X   X X X X X X

X X X X X X

X   X X X X X X

X X X X X X

X   X X X X X X

X X X X X X

X X X X X X X X X X

X X X X X X X X X X

X X X X X X X X X X

X X X X X X X X X X

X X X X X X X X X X

X X X X X X X X X X

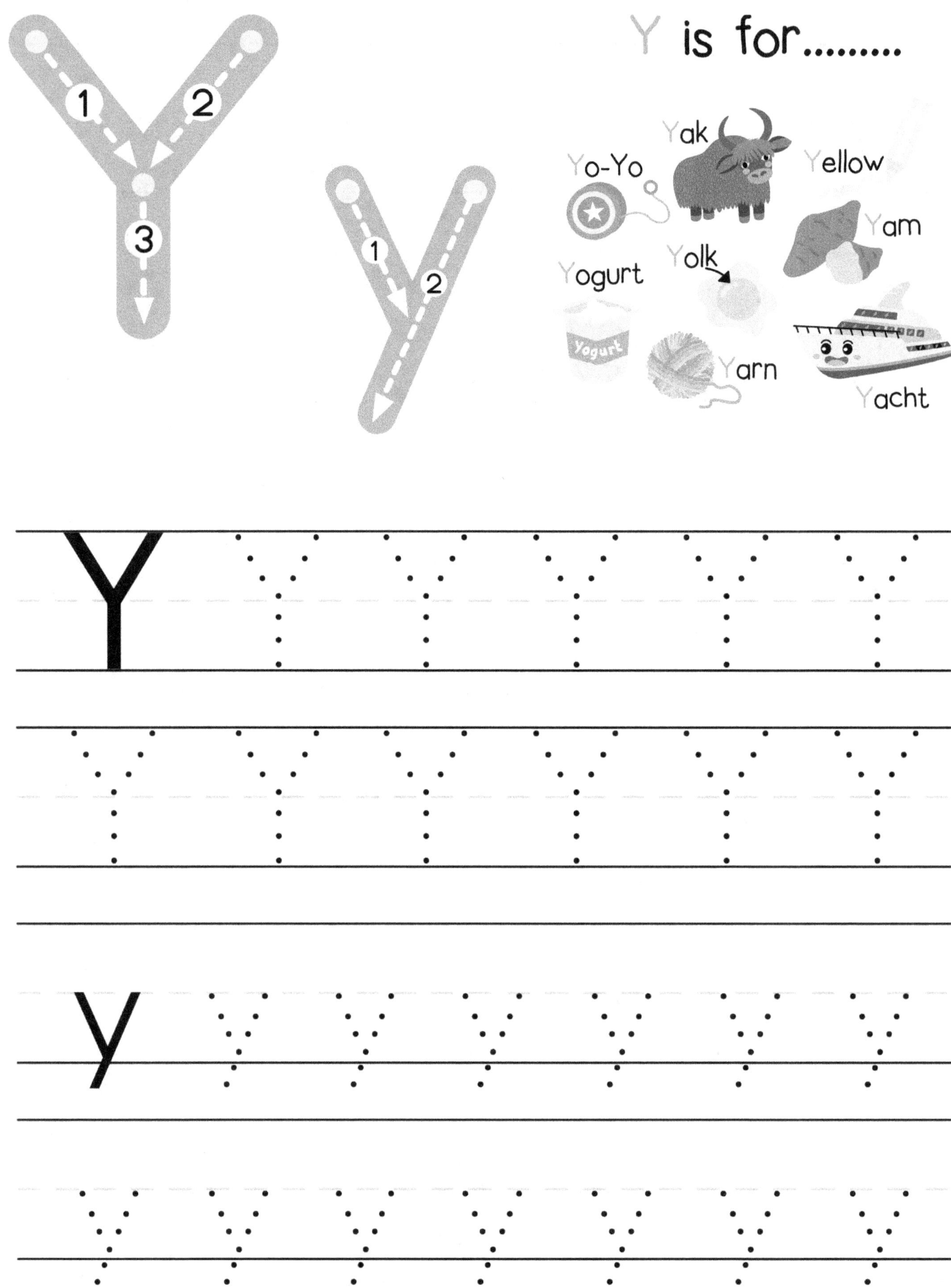

Y is for........
Yak
Yo-Yo
Yellow
Yam
Yogurt
Yolk
Yarn
Yacht

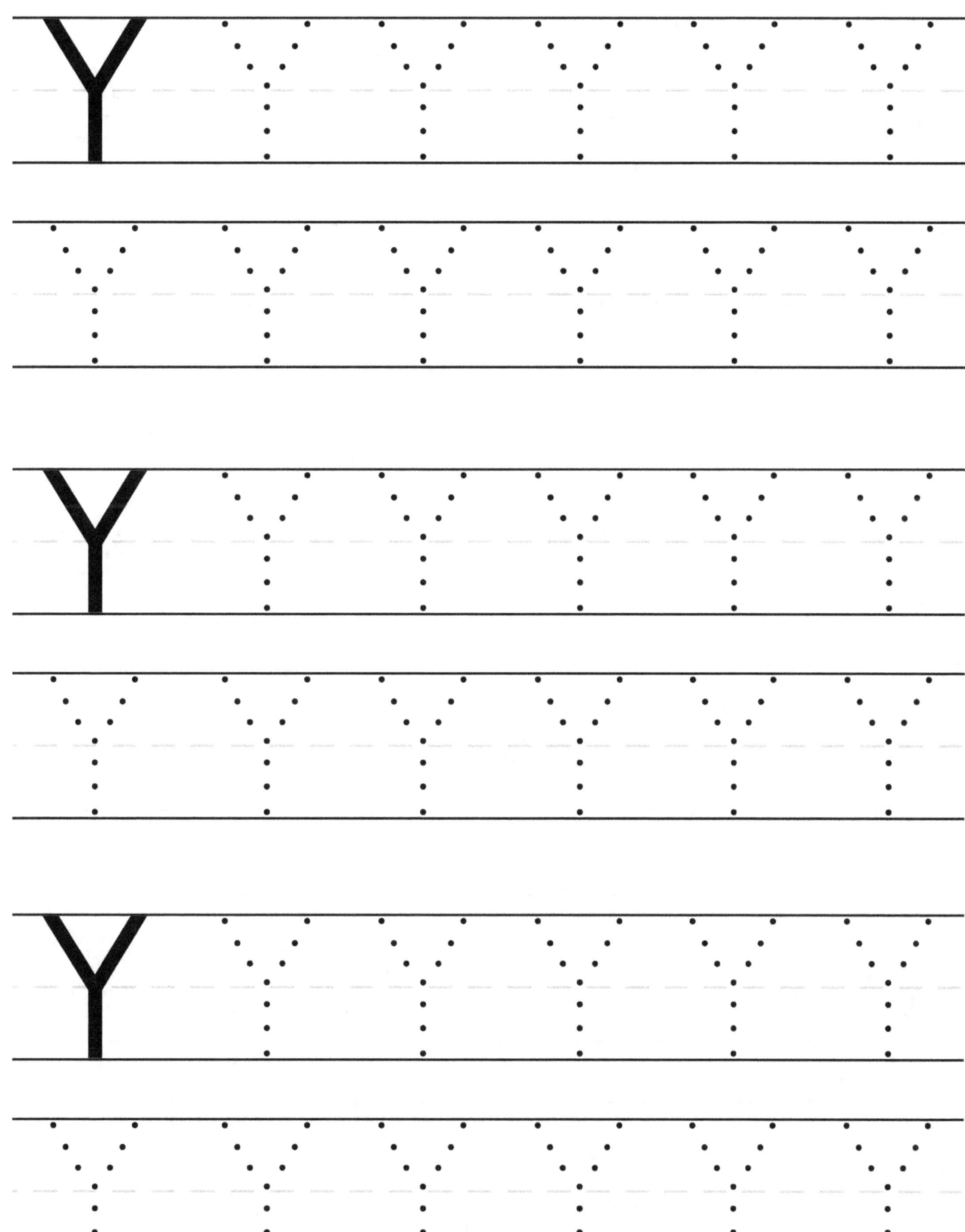

y

y

y

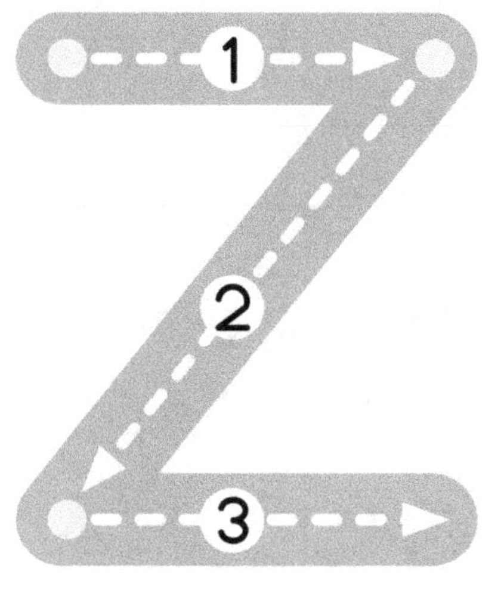

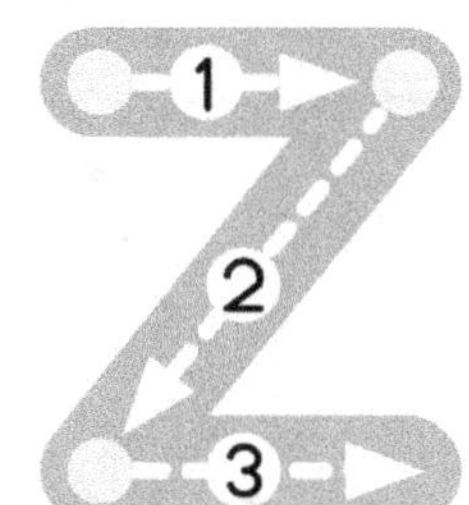

z is for.........
Zucchini
Zebra
Zoom
Zigzag
Zipper
Zero
Zebu
Zodiac
Zeppelin

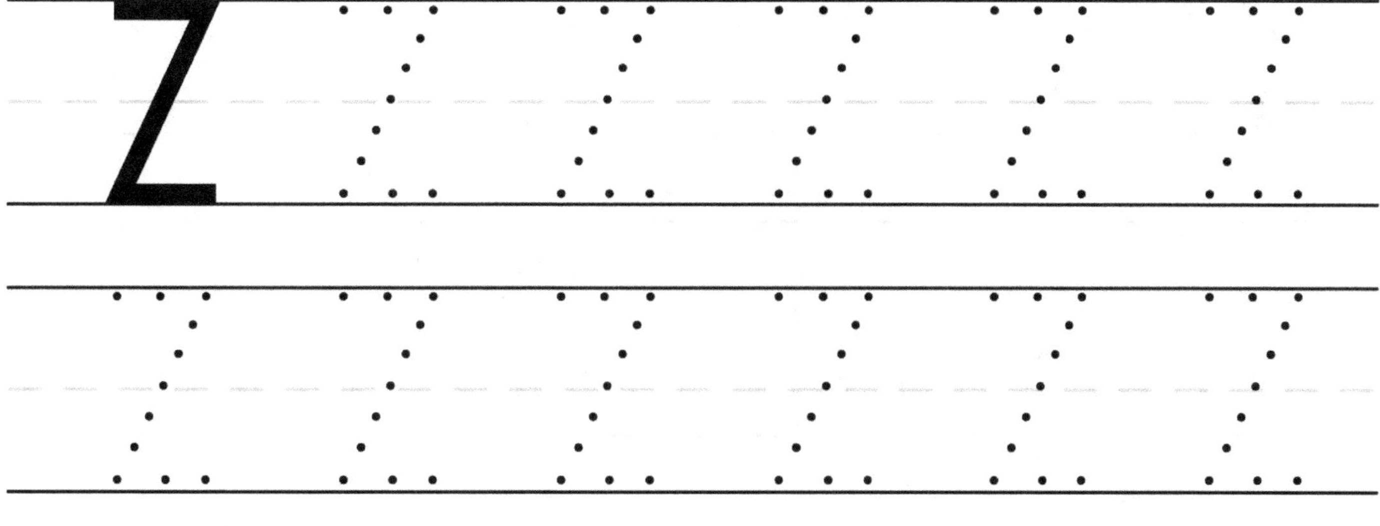

Z

Z

Z

Z

Z

Z

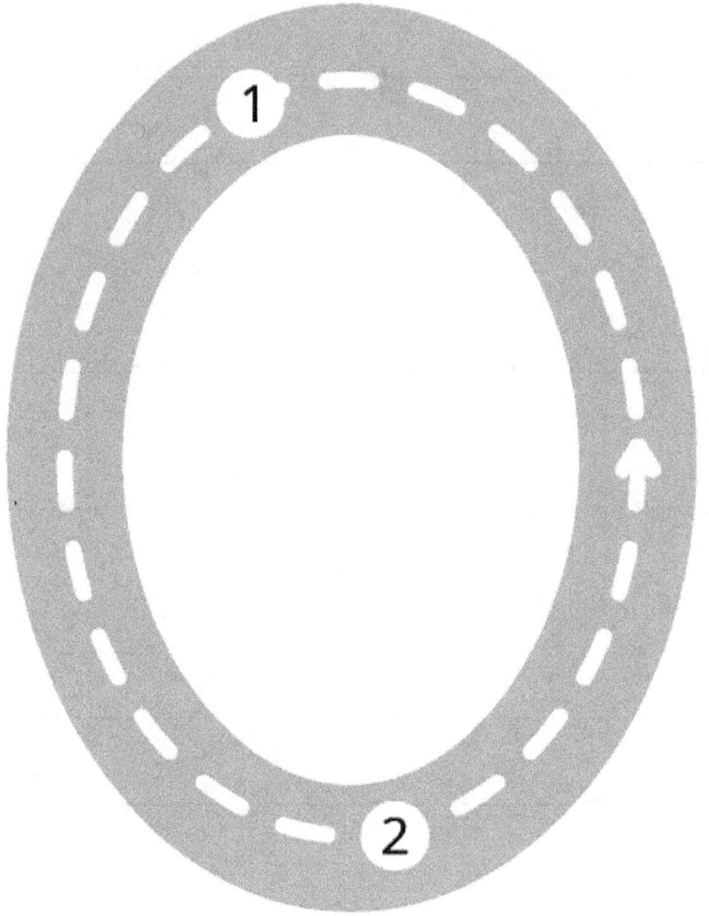

Zero

0 Zero

1
2
One

One

Two

2 Two

2 2 2 2 2

Three

3 Three

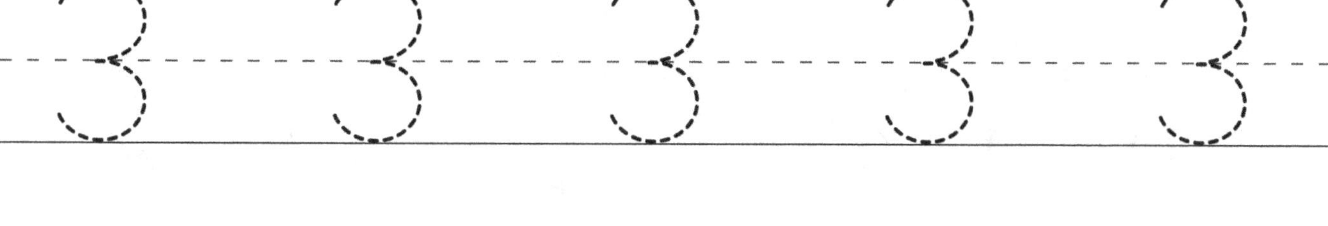

Four

4 Four

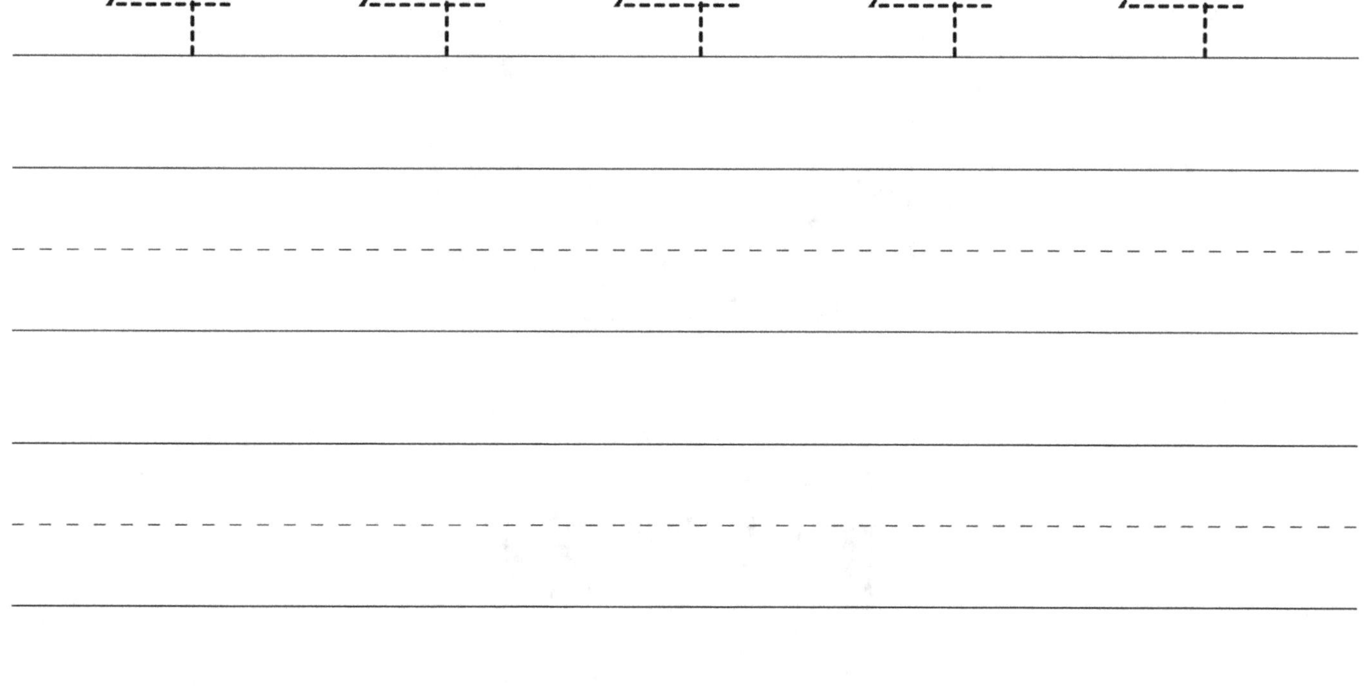

Five

5 Five

²↓ ¹→
5₃

5 5 5 5 5

Six

6 Six

6 6 6 6 6

1
2
Seven

7 Seven

Eight

8 Eight

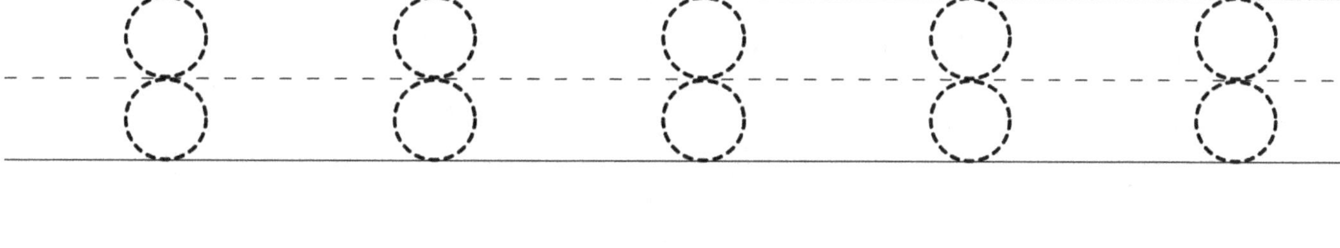

Nine

9 Nine

COLOR BY NUMBERS

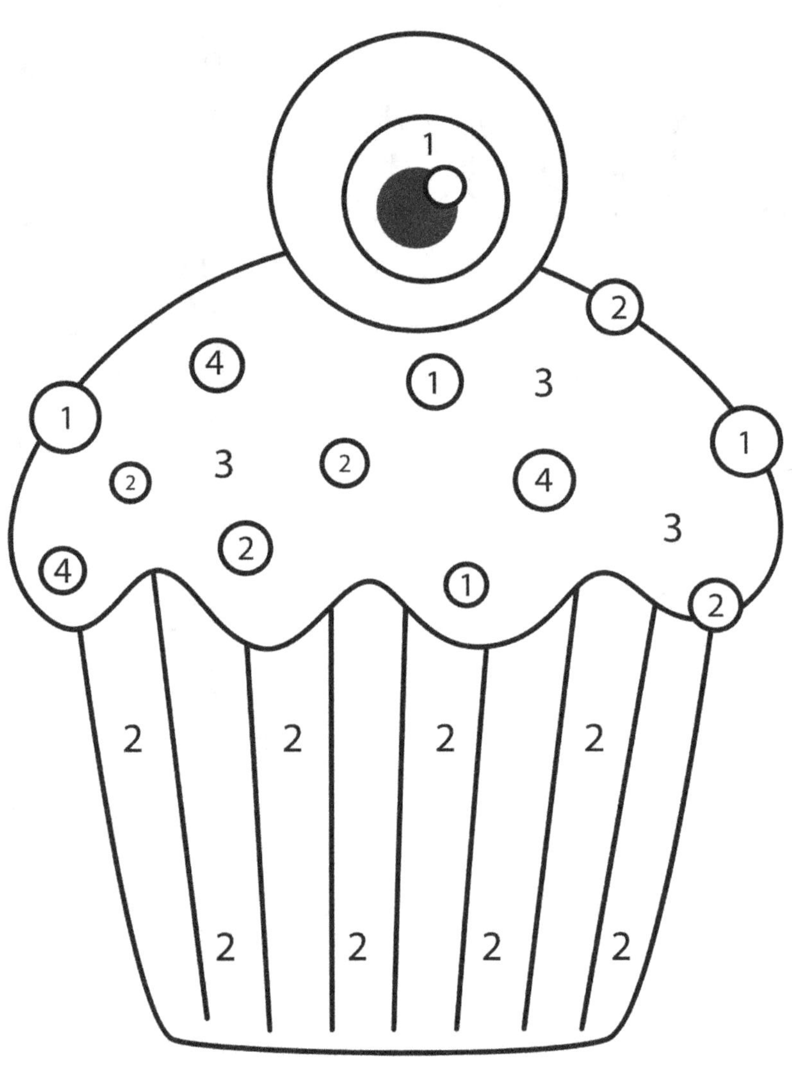

COLOR BY NUMBERS

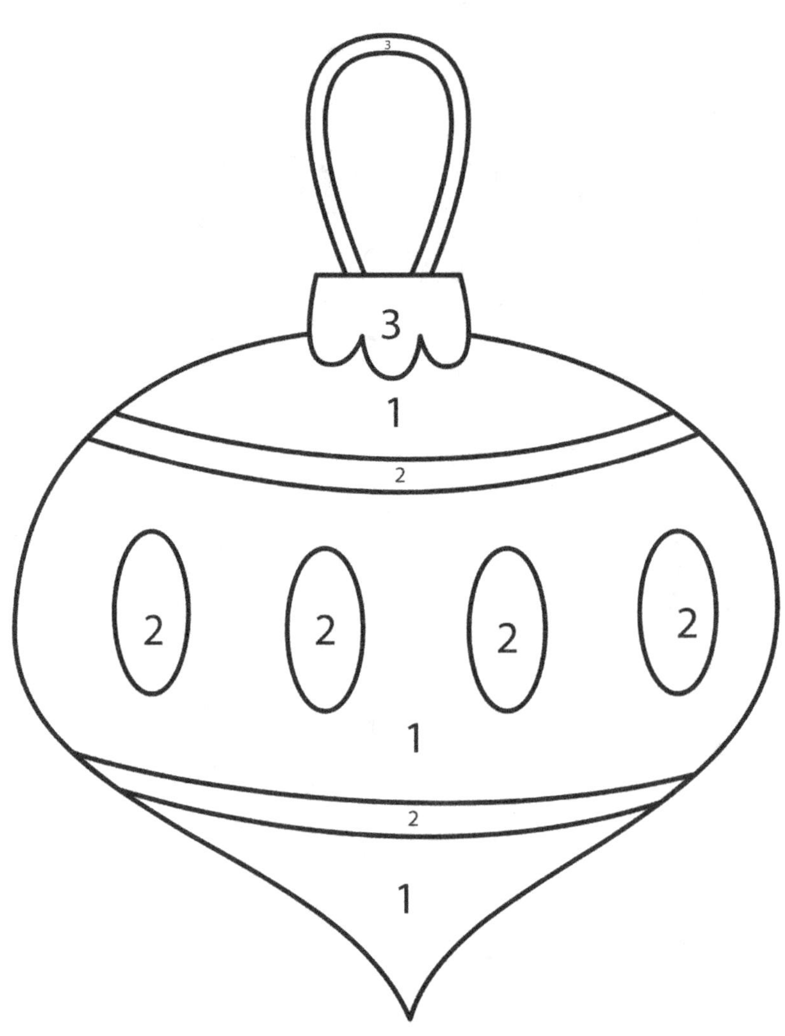

1 - 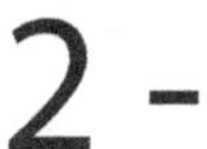   3 -

2 - 

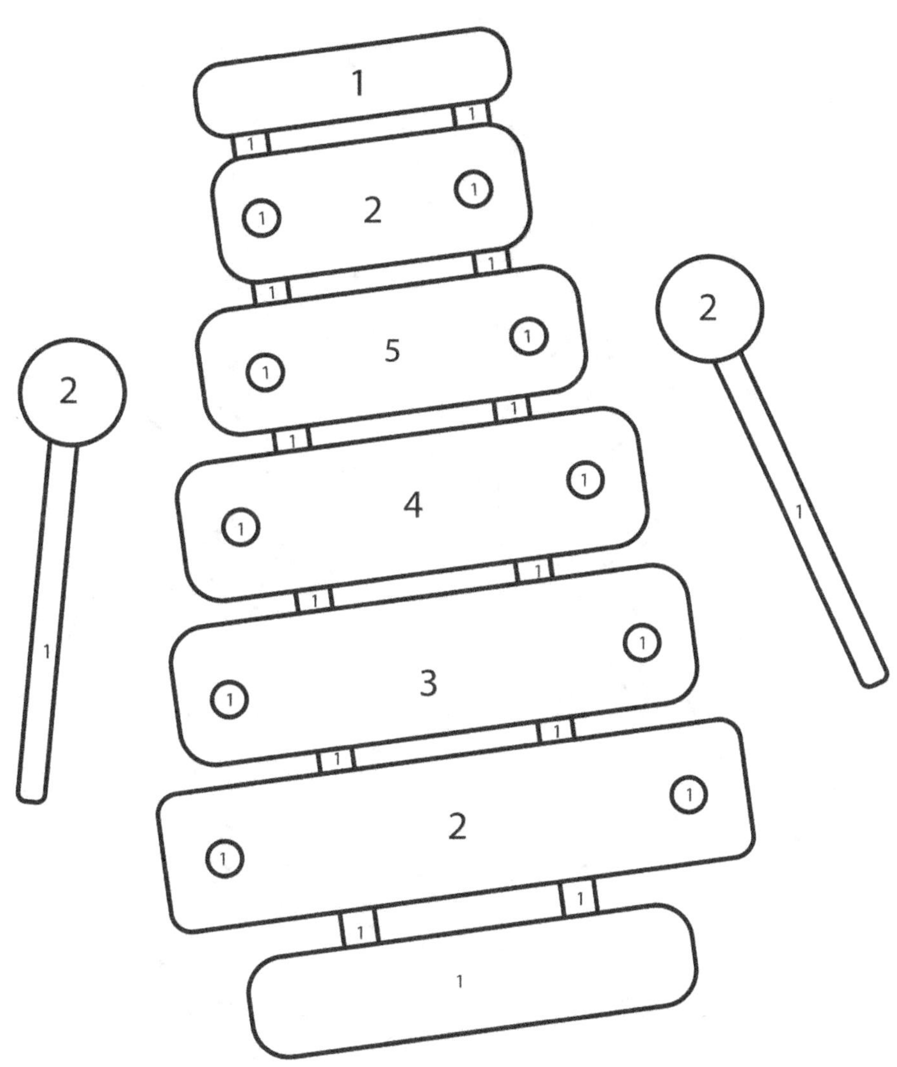

1 -

3 -

5 -

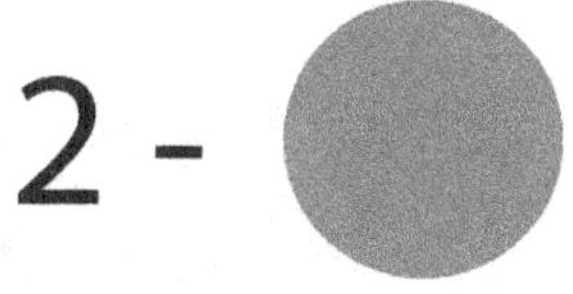

COLOR BY NUMBERS

COLOR BY NUMBERS

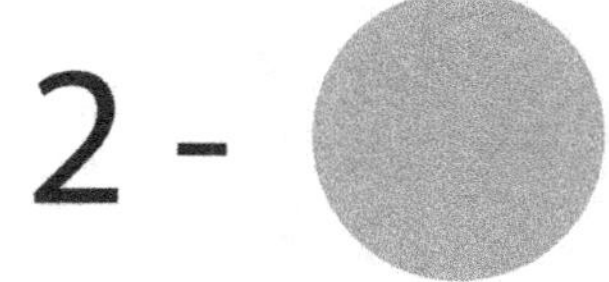

COLOR BY NUMBERS

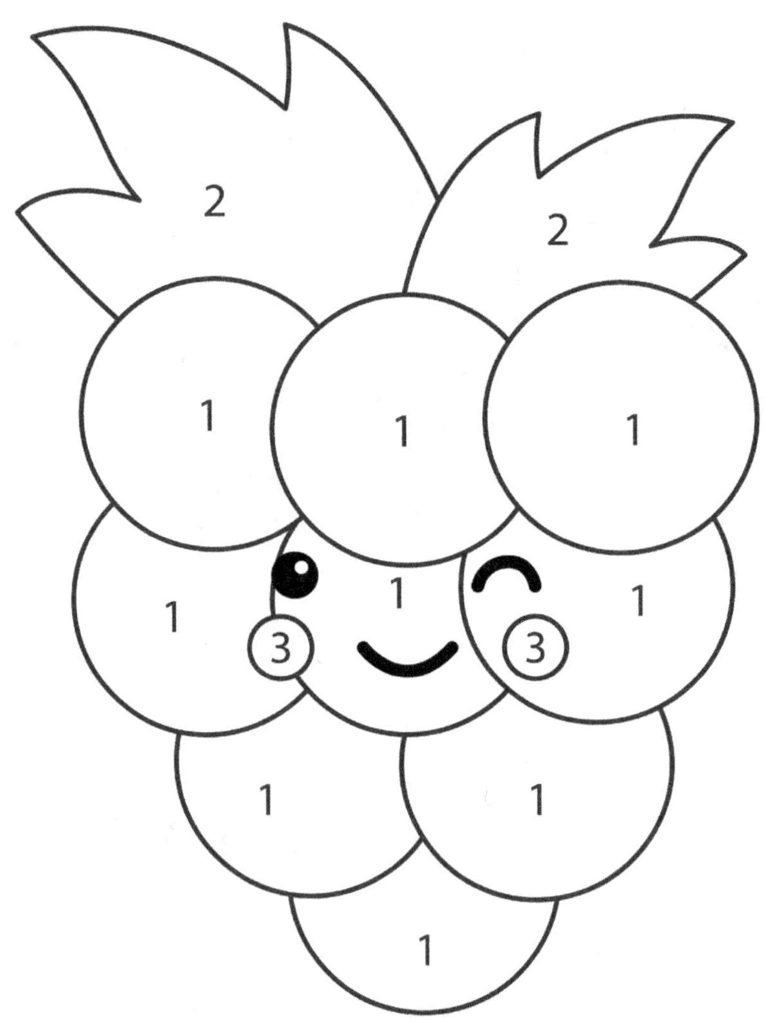

COLOR BY NUMBERS

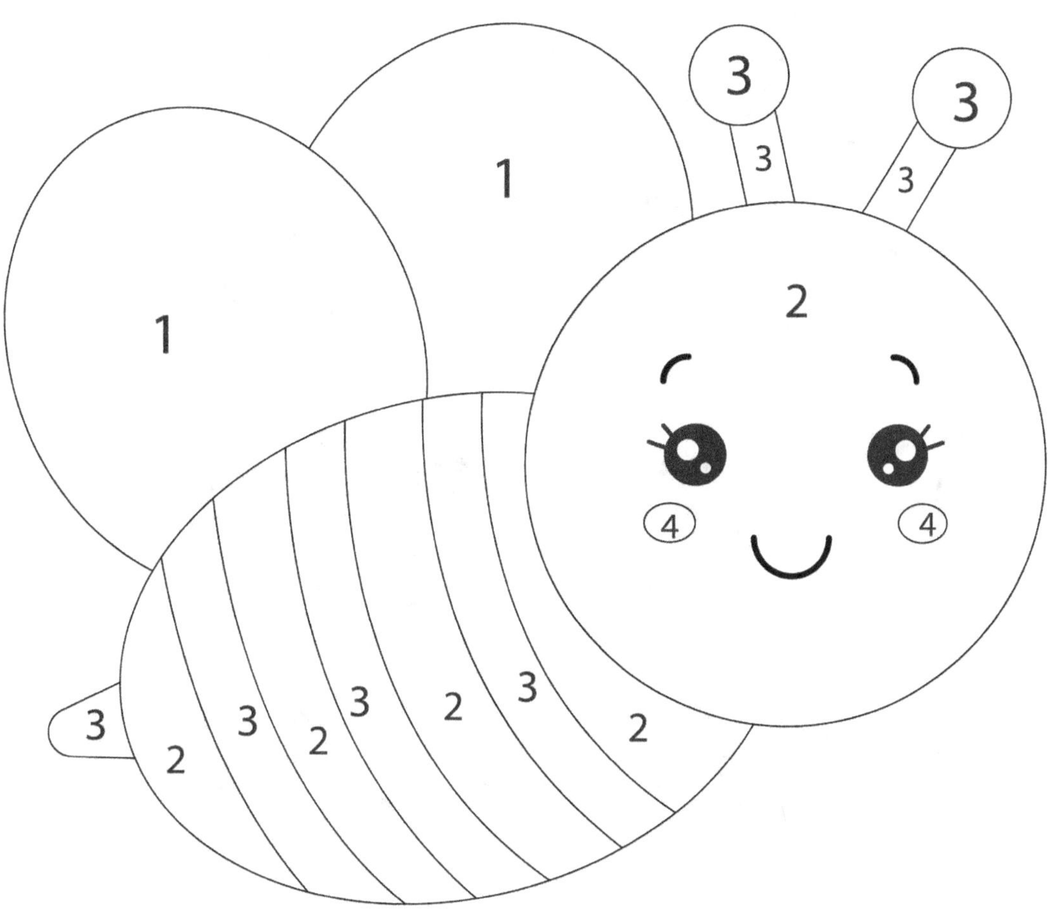

1 -

2 -

3 -

4 -

1 -

2 -

3 -

4 -

COLOR BY NUMBERS

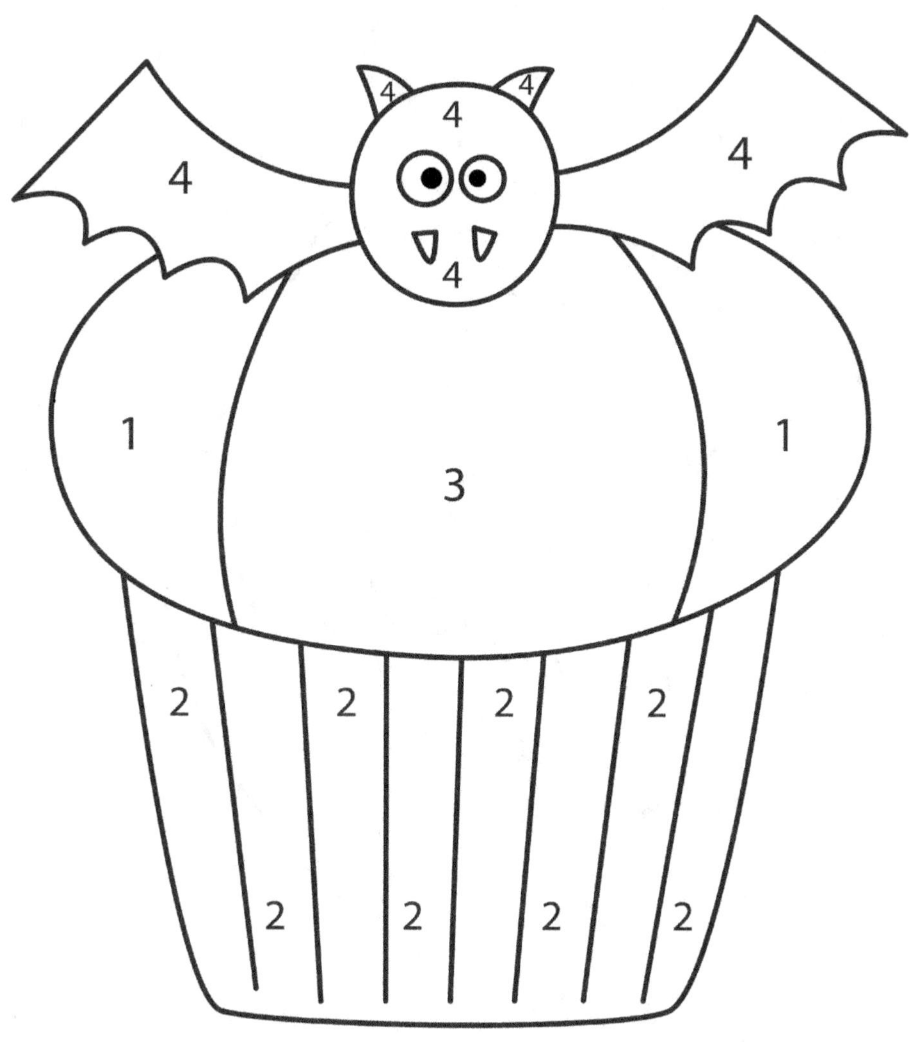

1 -

2 -

3 -

4 -

COLOR BY NUMBERS

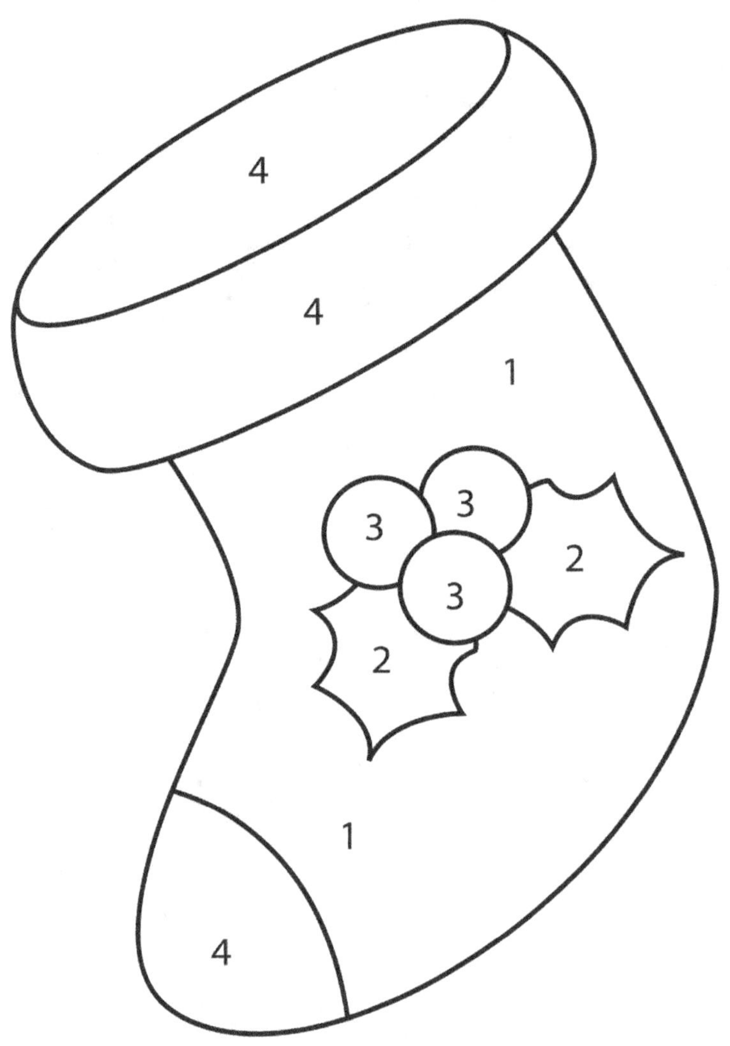

1 -

3 -

2 -

4 -